NEW DIRECTIONS FOR CHILD

William Damon, *Stanford University*
EDITOR-IN-CHIEF

Supportive Frameworks for Youth Engagement

Mimi Michaelson
Harvard University

Jeanne Nakamura
Claremont Graduate University

EDITORS

Number 93, Fall 2001

JOSSEY-BASS
A Wiley Company
www.josseybass.com

Supportive Frameworks for Youth Engagement
Mimi Michaelson, Jeanne Nakamura (eds.)
New Directions for Child and Adolescent Development, no. 93
William Damon, Editor-in-Chief

Microfilm copies of issues and articles are available in 16mm and 35mm, as well as microfiche in 105mm, through University Microfilms Inc., 300 North Zeeb Road, Ann Arbor, MI 48106.

ISSN 1520-3247 ISBN 0-7879-5777-1

New Directions for Child and Adolescent Development is part of The Jossey-Bass Education Series and is published quarterly by Jossey-Bass, 350 Sansome Street, San Francisco, CA 94104. Periodicals postage paid at San Francisco, California, and at additional mailing offices. Postmaster: Send address changes to New Directions for Child and Adolescent Development, Jossey-Bass, 989 Market Street, San Francisco, CA 94103-1741.

New Directions for Child and Adolescent Development is indexed in Biosciences Information Service, Current Index to Journals in Education (ERIC), Psychological Abstracts, and Sociological Abstracts.

Subscriptions cost $68.00 for individuals and $125.00 for institutions, agencies, and libraries.

Editorial correspondence should be sent to the Editor-in-Chief, William Damon, Stanford Center on Adolescence, Cypress Building C, Stanford University, Stanford, CA 94305.

Cover photograph by Wernher Krutein/PHOTOVAULT © 1990.

Jossey-Bass Web address: www.josseybass.com

Printed in the United States of America on acid-free recycled paper containing 100 percent recovered waste paper, of which at least 20 percent is postconsumer waste.

CONTENTS

EDITORS' NOTES

Creative work takes time, commitment, and sustained involvement. The lives of adults committed to domains like art, science, or social concerns have been widely studied. This volume extends these lines of investigation downward, exploring the phenomenon of engagement in adolescence and early adulthood. We are interested in what draws young people into an area of activity and what keeps them there—securing the foundation for what could be the starting point for larger discoveries.

In this volume we have gathered research that looks at which factors contribute to attracting young people to certain areas of work and, once they are there, sustain them. We draw primarily on two projects—the Good Work Project and the Alfred P. Sloan Study of Youth and Social Development. The Good Work Project is a collaboration among researchers at Claremont Graduate University, Harvard University, and Stanford University. The Sloan study was conducted by researchers at the University of Chicago. These projects differ in methodology and consider two spheres of creative work: work from the cultural sphere, like art or science, and work from the service sphere, like social involvement. We include work from both of these arenas, culture and service, because both have the potential to transform society.

The Research Projects

The Good Work Project focuses on interviews with adolescents and adults, selected for being "at promise" or highly successful in certain domains. The interviews probe the subjects' formative influences, goals, strategies, and obstacles. These interviews are supplemented with a forced-choice sorting task, in which subjects are required to prioritize values related to their work. These data, and the interviews in particular, give us personal insights and descriptions of factors that contribute to ongoing involvement in a domain.

The editors wish to thank the three principal investigators of the Good Work Project—Mihaly Csikszentmihalyi, William Damon, and Howard Gardner—as well as Barbara Schneider, a principal investigator of the Alfred P. Sloan Study of Youth and Social Development, for their continued support. We would also like to thank the members of the research teams at the three universities, especially Anne Gregory, who contributed to the project from the beginning. The Creativity in Later Life Project was supported by the Spencer Foundation. The Good Work Project was made possible by the generous support of the Carnegie Corporation of New York, the Christian A. Johnson Endeavor Foundation, the William and Flora Hewlett Foundation, the Louise and Claude Rosenberg Jr. Family Foundation, and the John Templeton Foundation. The Study of Youth and Social Development was conducted with the generous support of the Alfred P. Sloan Foundation.

The Alfred P. Sloan Study of Youth and Social Development lends insight into the subjective experience of involvement, using the Experience Sampling Method (ESM) to collect self-reports of everyday experience from adolescents. This longitudinal research provides firsthand data on felt experience over time, adding both experiential and developmental components to our understanding of ongoing interest and sustained involvement.

Chapters in This Volume

The first two chapters provide theoretical background that serves as a context for the empirical discussions.

Chapter One introduces the notion of "vital engagement" in order to suggest the kind of participation in the adult world toward which young people may be moving. In vital engagement the relationship between an individual and a sphere, like science or civil rights, is characterized by the presence of both absorption and felt significance. People can be vitally engaged in any sphere of life. In line with other contributions to this volume, the chapter draws illustrations from people engaged in cultural and social spheres.

Chapter Two focuses on the social sphere and proposes a framework of moral action. This chapter considers the notion of "moral giftedness," or exemplary social engagement, in light of literature on gifted youth and moral exemplars. A hypothetical portrait of a highly engaged young activist, which is constructed in the chapter, suggests features one might expect to see in a socially engaged young person.

In the remaining chapters we turn our attention to empirical studies from the research projects. We begin with research focused on service. Chapter Three describes a study of socially involved youth from the Good Work Project, identifying factors that motivate and sustain social commitment in a group of Albert Schweitzer Fellows. This chapter highlights the influence of role models, family, and other early experiences as well as the support of the fellowship program itself.

Chapter Four looks at a younger group of subjects (adolescents in middle and high school) and at possible precursors to community involvement. Using the Sloan study's ESM data, the authors highlight the relationship between the subjective experience of challenge in early adolescents and later cooperative behavior. Moderate challenge in daily life is found to be associated with participation in cooperative activities.

In the final two chapters, similar age comparisons are carried out in science and math. In Chapter Five, which focuses on a group of young adults (ages twenty-four to thirty-six) already committed to work in science, we see how mentorship affects young scientists. This Good Work study describes the impact of mentorship at two different moments in a scientific career. Certain kinds of mentoring foster scientific engagement in one generation and may facilitate an ongoing cycle of mentorship; that is, those who were well mentored may in turn go on to mentor others successfully.

Chapter Six describes factors that might channel interest into a scientific career. The authors look at the relationship between engagement in high school math and science classes and later academic performance and choice of college major, using data from the Sloan study. High engagement is found to be a good predictor of school performance, educational persistence, and career commitment.

These studies help us consider the importance of factors that may support ongoing commitment to an area of work—cultural or service work. Looking at adolescents and adults engaged in different forms of work, the authors have asked important questions about the elements and mechanisms that make a difference in how one pursues or develops an ongoing interest. They ask how felt significance, continuing interest, challenge, or the influence of mentors or role models sparks or sustains engagement in a domain. A glimpse at the relative importance of these different elements makes us question the relationships among them and how they may or may not work in concert. For example, how do challenge and mentoring mesh? These and additional questions appear as we look more closely at how young people embark on meaningful and creative work.

Mimi Michaelson
Jeanne Nakamura
Editors

MIMI MICHAELSON is currently a doctoral student at Harvard University and was the senior project manager for the Good Work Project at Harvard.

JEANNE NAKAMURA is research director at the Quality of Life Research Center, Claremont Graduate University.

1

Vital engagement, an absorbing and meaningful relationship between self and world, can be found in any sphere of life. This chapter describes the general phenomenon of vital engagement in adulthood to suggest what may lie ahead for engaged youth.

The Nature of Vital Engagement in Adulthood

Jeanne Nakamura

It is an abiding hope of concerned adults that young people will find goals to which they can devote themselves with genuine passion, pursuits in which they can become vitally engaged. It is important to ask how such engagement is, and thus might more often be, kindled in childhood or adolescence. This chapter focuses on a more basic question, however—what it means to be vitally engaged at all. It draws on interviews with adults who have long histories of vital engagement, in order to glean not so much what these individuals can recall about their youth but what they can communicate about their current activity, in which the phenomenon of vital engagement is clearly seen. The lives of these exemplars provide a glimpse of the possibilities that adulthood holds out to engaged youth.

The first section of the chapter introduces the notion of vital engagement, defined as an absorbing and meaningful relationship to the world. The second section discusses how relationships evolve so that the two aspects of vital engagement, absorption and subjective meaning, come together. This is neither a comprehensive review of the literature nor a report on research. Rather, the goal is to develop a picture of this form of positive experience.

Most of our field's attention has focused on understanding either normative experience or ways in which lives are distorted by histories of adversity or

---

The Creativity in Later Life Project was supported by the Spencer Foundation. The Good Work Project studies that this chapter draws on were conducted with support from the William and Flora Hewlett Foundation, the Carnegie Corporation of New York, and the John Templeton Foundation.

pathological societal conditions. Comparatively little research has focused on positive experience, despite the manifest need for a fuller understanding of it (Seligman and Csikszentmihalyi, 2000). The concept of vital engagement addresses the latter need. Although many forms of engagement with the world have been examined (for example, vocation, learning, friendship, love, faith, aesthetic appreciation, service work, creativity), each has typically been treated alone. The notion of vital engagement is intended to offer a way of thinking about and drawing together a whole category of positive experience.

Context of the Discussion

Constructing a relationship to the world that is meaningful and involving has been viewed as a positive developmental outcome in humanistic, existential, and other psychological theories. The particular notion of vital engagement stands at the intersection of two traditions.

One is the experientialist tradition, whose clearest precursor is the pragmatist philosophical psychology of Dewey (1930, 1934), James ([1890] 1981), and Mead (1934). Whereas much recent psychological research is cognitive in focus, the experientialist tradition attends to *experience* (Dewey, 1938)—the interaction between the whole person and the environment (compare Magnusson and Stattin, 1998)—and the person's *subjective experience* of these interactions (Csikszentmihalyi, 1975; Csikszentmihalyi and Csikszentmihalyi, 1988). People's allocation of attention, construction of meaning, and formation of goals are studied in the context of their ongoing relationship to the world. (For examples of work on positive experience specifically, see Csikszentmihalyi and Rathunde, 1998; Csikszentmihalyi and Robinson, 1990; Csikszentmihalyi and Rochberg-Halton, 1981; and Inghilleri, 1999.) A particular way of interacting with the world characterizes vital engagement.

The second tradition is the study of lives, which originated with Murray (White, 1963) and Allport (1937) and has been enriched in subsequent decades by life course and narrative studies (Cohler, 1982; McAdams, 1993; Neugarten, 1969). It attends to the organization of experience across the life course—that is, continuity and change in the person's relationship to the world—and thus complements the experientialist focus on the organization of experience at one point in life. (For examples of work on engaged lives specifically, see Colby and Damon, 1992; Daloz, Keen, Keen, and Parks, 1996; and Csikszentmihalyi, 1996.) Vital engagement is a particular way of being related to the world over time.

The concept of vital engagement has its roots in Dewey's notions (1913, 1934, 1938) of *artistic-aesthetic experience* and *interest.* In Dewey's analysis (1934, p. 280) of art as "the ideal for all experience," he described the possibility of transactions in daily life between self and world in which the person feels vital and fully alive because he is wholly absorbed in the experience. In this artistic-aesthetic experience there is "active and alert commerce with the world; at its height it signifies complete interpenetration of self and the world of objects and events" (Dewey, 1934, p. 19). In interest the "whole-hearted identification with what one is doing" finds a specific focus (Dewey, 1913, p. 80). Interest characterizes the person's relationship to some particular aspect of the world that attracts and holds attention because of its felt significance: the self becomes "engaged, engrossed, or entirely taken up with some activity because of its recognized worth" (Dewey, 1913, p. 17).

Consistent with the study of lives (Allport, 1937), this chapter highlights the notion of a relationship that endures over time. In the research literature some recent interest concepts are compatible with this emphasis, notably Rathunde's *abiding interest* (1995) and Fink's *fully developed interest* (1991). However, interest is defined in divergent ways by contemporary researchers (Renninger, Hidi, and Krapp, 1992). To avoid ambiguity and to communicate the intended generality of the phenomenon, this chapter introduces the term *vital engagement.* This term encompasses not only sustained engagement with things and with spheres of activity, which *interest* connotes, but in addition, engagement with another person (such as a friend, spouse, or colleague), with groups (such as teammates, one's children, a community, or the poor), with causes and concerns—in fact, with any *object,* or aspect of the world.

Vital Engagement

To ground the discussion that follows, consider two exemplars of long-term vital engagement, a social activist and a scientist. In both cases the notion of vital engagement as a sustained relationship is particularly vivid because an origin account is provided for the current relationship.

For example, referring to childhood, the social activist recalls:

> [I remember hearing from the kitchen the] coffee pot percolating, and my parents and their friends talking about what I thought [of] as . . . the big, important things, you know? And even though I didn't know exactly what they were talking about, I found those memories of that *intensity* of their involvement, of their *caring* about what was happening in the society at large, and their effort to found this church. . . . It all had to do with democracy, in effect. It all had to do with inclusivity. And democratic process was the *core* of it. What was fair, what was just . . . *of course* one wanted to be part of the answer. One wanted to have a life that had some meaning, that you were aligning yourself with something that was better than what had been. . . . I never had to sort of "come to" that. I mean, that was just the nature of what I lived within [Good Work Project interviews, 1997–2000].

Similarly, an astronomer recalls a lifelong, uninterrupted fascination with the stars:

> We moved to Washington when I was ten and I had a bed under a window that faced north, and I started watching the sky and just got mesmerized by watching the stars . . . and that really for several years was probably the most important thing in my life other than going to school.
>
> The curiosity of how the universe works—I still have this feeling. When I am out observing at a very dark site on a clear night and I look at the stars, I still really wonder how you could do anything but be an astronomer, and that's the truth. How could you live looking up at those stars and just not spend your life learning about what's going on? [Creativity in Later Life Project interviews, 1990–1995].

As these passages illustrate, vital engagement describes a particular way of being related to the world characterized by both felt meaning (subjective significance) and experiences of enjoyed absorption (flow). It is a relationship in the everyday sense: the person feels connected to an aspect of the world (such as the cause of democracy or the stars), and this connection has been sustained over some period of time rather than being a fleeting event.

In vital engagement the participation in the world is intense and positive. These qualities characterize both the enduring relationship and immediate experience. The relationship is intense in that the person's sense of being connected is strong, and positive in that it brings together subjectively important aspects of self and world. Immediate experience is intense in that the person becomes completely caught up in the interaction; it is positive in that these interactions with the world are absorbing and infused with felt significance, or meaning.

This chapter focuses on vital engagement in particular self-object relationships—extended participation in specific spheres that a person finds engaging. Space limitations preclude discussion of two other related phenomena: construction of an engaged life through the overall ensemble of enduring relationships to the world that a person cultivates and general attitudes, such as curiosity, that favor a person's engagement in their every encounter with the world.

A Relationship Between Self and World. Consider more closely the characterization of vital engagement as a relationship between self and world. Such relationships are particularly significant because they transform both the self and the object. As Dewey (1934) put it, they work a *double change*: they are a means of self-realization and simultaneously a means of changing the world.

If a person's relationship to the world is vitally engaging, this is at least in part because it involves aspects of the *self* that the individual values: the person's cherished goals in life; their guiding beliefs and commitments; impulses, gifts, and strengths that they embrace. A woman who has worked for more than thirty years meeting the basic needs of the poor described this work as expressing her deep religious faith and making use of her "highest capacity"—love and generosity toward others (Colby and Damon, 1992, p. 227). A lifelong writer sees poetry as realizing a "powerful impulse within" and a "strong gift for making poems" (Creativity in Later Life Project interviews, 1990–1995).

Any given individual is probably more receptive to some aspects of the world than others. Poets speak of a special receptivity to language, activists of heightened sensitivity to people's suffering, and so on. Although we may leave uncultivated those strengths that we ourselves do not value, vital engagement tends to be encouraged along lines of talent both by the enjoyment of mastering challenges and by the rewards of social approval.

Vital engagement takes the person beyond the self; it is a relationship to some aspect of the world, to an object. This might be a tangible object, such as another person, a thing that one creates or transforms, or a possession. However, the category encompasses any object of attention and energy that engages a person, including a concept, a cause, or a symbolic domain. An object is defined by the person's focus in the attentional and experiential field: numbers and axioms for a mathematician, a principle (such as democracy) for an activist. From the person's standpoint, the object defines a set of opportunities for action.

Immediate Experience. What is the self-object experience like on those occasions when the individual is fully engaged in the moment? The experience begins when something—a problem, a fascination—stimulates conscious perception rather than routine response (Dewey, 1930). Resolving the problem or pursuing the fascination structures the person's investment of attention and energy.

The experience is carried forward by a dialectic of *doing,* or action, and *undergoing,* or the taking in of the consequences of prior action (Dewey, 1934). When an individual is thus engaged (whether with a partner in conversation, a half-painted canvas, a scientific puzzle, or something else), the doing is attentive action rather than the mere enacting of habit. The undergoing is the conscious perceiving of the object, in contrast to the bare recognition of the object that may serve a person well in routine activity. Undergoing constitutes a means of developing the unfolding experience with a view toward what is to be done next. The present moment is organically related to the immediate past and immediate future when a person is fully engaged.

Flow. The subjective experience of absorption, or *flow*, is associated with this dialectic of action and perception. Research on activities engaged in because of their experiential rewards has delineated the subjective experience of full involvement (Csikszentmihalyi, 1975, 1990, 1997; Csikszentmihalyi and Csikszentmihalyi, 1988).

Enjoyable absorption is favored by certain structural conditions of the self-object relationship, including clarity of goals, immediacy of feedback, and a match between the person's capacities for action and the challenges found in the relationship (Csikszentmihalyi, 1975, 1997). When fully involved, completely caught up in one's interaction with the world, one experiences a state of flow. The flow state is distinguished by intense and focused concentration, a merging of action and awareness and loss of self-consciousness, a sense that one will be able to handle the situation, a distorted impression of how quickly time has passed, and an experience of the activity as intrinsically rewarding in and of itself, regardless of the outcome. As one poet put it, "[Y]ou're right in the work, you lose your sense of time, you're completely enraptured, you're completely caught up in what you're doing" (Csikszentmihalyi, 1996, p. 121).

Felt Significance. Absorption is one aspect of the subjective phenomenology of engagement; the other is *felt significance.* An experience that draws a person into participation in the world yet holds little felt significance may be briefly absorbing but is not vitally engaging. That is, involving activities are vitally engaging if the relationship is experienced as meaningful, as being important and mattering to the individual.

Like flow, felt significance is associated with certain structural conditions. The key condition is the connection or integration of the self with something that is valued. Felt significance may be due to the inherent worth that the person ascribes to an object of attention and action. For an activist working with the poor, their lives are "precious." It may be due to ends that are valued, to which the immediate experience connects the self. For a biologist, environmental research is a way of "dealing with real world problems" (Creativity in Later Life Project interviews, 1990–1995). It may derive from the relationship's place in an encompassing worldview or theory of reality, as in the grounding of service work in a religious belief system. As mentioned earlier, the person's relationship with the world in each case recruits valued aspects of the self, and this also is a source of felt significance.

The engaged individual's attitude toward the object is serious because the relationship matters and playful because interactions are inherently enjoyable. The balance of seriousness and playfulness, discussed by Dewey (1910), was also observed in optimal talent development during youth (Csikszentmihalyi, Rathunde, and Whalen, 1993). There, seriousness was associated specifically with perceived relevance to long-term goals; in mature engagement, it may stem from various sources of meaning, including the object's inherent value or a person's sense of calling.

Engagement over Time. Vital engagement is distinct from the transient subjective state of being in flow, absorbed, engrossed. Though it occasions intense flow experiences, vital engagement is a self-object relationship that endures over time. It reflects and supports a sustained channeling of attention and energy in a particular direction. A dynamic balancing of commitment and openness means that the relationship is characterized by both continuity and change (Colby and Damon, 1992). Relationships vary in duration, sometimes lasting throughout a lifetime. A scientist observed, "It's like an enduring marriage. It matures, the relationship. . . . Take something that intrigues you, and intrigue can mature into familiarity and excitement, and can—that can mature into a lifelong passion" (Creativity in Later Life Project interviews, 1990–1995).

Creators and activists describe not only experiences of flow but also phases of work that are strenuous or wearisome and fallow periods in which little is accomplished (Colby and Damon, 1992; Csikszentmihalyi, 1990, 1996). Because both a lived past and desired future richly inform present experience and because any complex object represents a beckoning sphere of possibility, vital engagement can survive these periods when things do not go well.

Sustained engagement has distinctive qualities. In particular, the relationship to the object grows to have a moral-affective dimension. The engaged person's attention and action come to be characterized by an attitude of care because the activity matters (Dewey, 1934); the object has subjective worth. Care is highlighted as a central quality of the moral exemplars studied by Colby and Damon (1992). A missionary working to feed homeless children professed, "[I have] a love for these people that I myself don't understand" (Colby and Damon, 1992, p. 47). The attitude is not unique to individuals whose work serves other people. For engaged artists, scientists, and others, attention to the object is total and appreciative. Action directed toward the object is caring and solicitous. Historian Natalie Davis provides an example: "I think there's partly something maternal in me with regard to the past. . . . It's a sense of those lives that were lived and felt and had their own intent and mustn't be lost or go unmarked. . . . I care about making heard the voices of people who have stood outside" (Abelove and others, 1983, p. 113).

The development of an attitude of care suggests one reason why vital engagement matters beyond its significant intrinsic rewards: it affects the quality of a person's impact on the object. In addition, happiness and a sense that life has meaning are "by-products" of one's engagement with the world (Yalom, 1980; see also Csikszentmihalyi and Rochberg-Halton, 1981; Jackson, 1998; Weisskopf-Joelson, 1968). They tend to be attained when pursued indirectly by participating in the world, rather than when they are adopted as deliberate goals.

Research has shown that flow, or absorption, occurs when a person's capacities for action are stretched. As capacities increase, challenges must correspondingly rise if the person is to remain absorbed; sustained engagement thus fosters growth (Csikszentmihalyi, 1990; Massimini and Delle Fave, 2000). Moreover, from at least some therapeutic perspectives, vital engagement can defuse existential questions about the meaning of life, taking away their urgency, even if it cannot provide a direct answer to them

(Yalom, 1980). It does so by integrating the self with something beyond itself and giving direction to a person's life.

Creative Work and Service Work as Examples of Vital Engagement

Vital engagement is possible in many different spheres. A factor obscuring this phenomenon is the variation across spheres along other dimensions and the apparent absence of some features of vital engagement in particular domains. Consider creative work and service work more closely. These two kinds of vital engagement appear dramatically different in certain respects. However, data from two studies of adult exemplars indicate that vital engagement characterizes both groups, even in ways that might be unexpected (Colby and Damon, 1992; Csikszentmihalyi, 1996).

The moral exemplars studied by Colby and Damon (1992) crystallize what it means to be vitally engaged with the social sphere (Daloz, Keen, Keen, and Parks, 1996). Those committed to social action illustrate with great clarity the cathexis of something beyond the self and an attitude of care toward the object manifest in attention and action. Perhaps more surprisingly, Colby and Damon reported that both "helpers" and "reformers" (Carlson, 1982) experienced flow in their work, joining playfulness with seriousness in their attitude toward it. Rather than effacing the self in their service to others, lifelong activists find self-realization through their work, doing so in the "medium of action" (Andrews, 1991, p. 156).

Predictably, moral exemplars experience their work as profoundly meaningful. Frequently, a larger framework of meaning (for example, a religious system) inspires and sustains their relationship to the world. In contrast, the obstacles to flow are apparent: the great uncertainty of success, the hardship and sacrifice entailed, the suffering seen, and the soberness of the undertaking (Andrews, 1991; Colby and Damon, 1992; Daloz, Keen, Keen, and Parks, 1996). Nevertheless, interviewing moral exemplars and observing them at work led Colby and Damon to conclude that they "enter the fray wholeheartedly" (p. 82), demonstrating "an enjoyment of the work that they are doing—whether it is fighting for racial justice, helping the poor, or working for peace" (p. 262), and that "their joyful absorption in their work is recognizable as the 'flow' experience" (p. 270).

The lifelong artists and scientists studied by Csikszentmihalyi (1996) illustrate what it means to be vitally engaged with the cultural sphere. Indeed, studies of creators consistently reveal a close association between sustained creative accomplishment and passionate engagement with a domain (Ochse, 1990). Artists and scientists exemplify the realization of the self through a cultural medium, the experience of deep absorption, or flow, and the joining of seriousness and playfulness in the attitude toward the object.

Less obviously perhaps, vitally engaged creators are carried outside of themselves via the relationship. Artists and scientists may lack the marked love for other people evidenced by moral exemplars (Colby and Damon, 1992); however, creators come to exhibit a corresponding care or solicitude toward the objects that do compel them. A musician stressed the importance of "respect" for the instrument: "[I]t has feelings. And if you cater to those feelings, emotionally—by that I mean even just with touch, and so forth—the piano will respond" (Creativity in Later Life Project interviews, 1990–1995).

Emergence of Absorption and Meaning

How does a person become vitally engaged with a particular object? In the most organic pathway to vital engagement, individuals experience an object as both significant and involving from early in their relationship with it. One may experience, from the outset, deep absorption in interactions with the object and a sense that it has inherent worth or significance. The astronomer described earlier, who can still recall becoming fascinated by the stars as a child, exemplifies this.

In the absence of this *attraction* (Renninger and Leckrone, 1991), or immediate response to the object itself, how does a relationship evolve that couples felt significance and experiences of absorption? How do people discover that interaction with an object absorbs them, and how do they find meaning in their relationship to some aspect of the world? This chapter highlights two sets of possible factors: the influence of others and the impact of a person's own experience. A more complete analysis would encompass other factors, including culture, society, and history.

Influence of Others. Socialization is one possible factor—growing up in an environment that places a high priority on pursuing what one enjoys, pursuing something that matters, or both. In a person's formative environment any of these priorities may be taken for granted as a way of relating to the world (Berger and Luckmann, 1966). One might be exposed to the general notion of vital engagement or to others' cathexis of the world at large (for example, a general curiosity about the world). Alternatively, one might be exposed to the idea of engagement, or to an example of it, in some particular sphere. The latter is illustrated by the influence of the parents' circle on the lifelong social activist described earlier.

Mentors, teachers, and other professionals who introduce an individual to a domain like art or science may model or otherwise convey a mode of participation in the endeavor that the younger person had not yet imagined (Bloom, 1985): a fullness of absorption in the activity, a sense that the work deeply matters, vital engagement. Individuals distant in time or space also may play an important role in stirring a person's desire for and vision of absorption, meaning, or sense of vocation in relationship to the world. Books and other cultural objects are a key medium of influence. Biographies and histories communicate how a specific endeavor can be an engaging enterprise—important and absorbing, even riveting.

Influence of Experience. An individual's own experience, particularly direct experience with art, science, service, or any other domain—the self-object interaction itself—is of course a primary pathway to the discovery that a sphere can be absorbing or meaningful. This can take a number of different forms.

In terms of discovering through experience what absorbs them, people are exposed to new possibilities for engagement in many ways. These include their own concerted efforts to become involved in an activity and their more diffuse explorations, the intercession of other individuals who introduce them to activities, the requirements of school, work, or other roles and statuses, and chance encounters.

Once brought into contact with the object, a variety of factors can hold people in a relationship long enough to develop the capacities for action that are required for flow, or absorption. Becoming vitally engaged with an object is favored to the extent that the investment of energy is not dictated by drives, cultural scripts, or other external demands but instead is emergently motivated (Csikszentmihalyi and Nakamura, 1999), influenced by comparing the subjective experience in the current activity to alternatives encountered in the past.

In terms of discovering *felt meaning* in what one does, direct experience leads a relationship to acquire subjective significance in at least two possible ways. It can acquire felt meaning through interactions with the world that are prior to and inspire involvement with the object. For example, a person may encounter an urgent existential problem in childhood or youth, such as experiencing the death of a loved one. As a result of this experience, a highly personal sense of significance may come to be ascribed to some domain—legal work, medicine, activism—because the person formulates it as a way of dealing with the experienced problem (Csikszentmihalyi and Beattie, 1979). More commonly, if a flow activity is pursued over a period of time, the individual comes to be integrated into a community, and experience becomes situated within a larger ongoing human project. In this way, an enjoyable activity gradually accrues felt meaning of increasing richness, through direct experience with the object.

Felt significance thus includes, but is certainly not exhausted by, transcendent purpose, which not every engaged individual avows. Although emergence of a sense of larger purpose is not inevitable, many of the factors described earlier can foster it. For example, as an illustration of how perceiving unintended consequences of one's experience can lead to a sense of larger purpose, consider a business executive who initially pursued his work "for some very narrow reasons" (Good Work Project interviews, 1997–2000): it was just a "really interesting" game. He recalls, "It probably wasn't until about ten years after that, when I finally had gotten a chance to create and run a business, that it really hit me that this isn't a game at all. . . . I don't think I was conscious that I was treating it as a game but I think that was the initial fascination." His company had developed and introduced a product, and he was "very proud" when it rapidly became "very, very successful." He had played the game well. Then he began to receive letters from customers; many were parents of sick children. "This product had mattered to them," he explains. "It changed things for them. It made their lives better. That really hit me." Looking back, he can vividly remember "when the reality of what businesses do as a human activity, with effects on people . . . became dramatically clear." Referring to that point in time, he says, "I think that was when I really fell in love with it." His enjoyment of the work's challenges continued—but now embedded within an emergent sense of its larger significance.

Not all individuals would respond to this experience by enlarging their relationship to the work, and chance clearly played a role in this case. The point is that the emergence of a sense of larger purpose was analogous to the process by which finding flow inspires an intention to repeat the enjoyable activity (Csikszentmihalyi and Nakamura, 1999). Whether by chance or some other means, if a person discovers that an activity can have an impact (can "matter") above and beyond the other rewards that it provides (in this case, the satisfaction of playing well), thereafter he or she can steer investment of attention and energy into things that have a larger good as a potential outcome.

Absorption and Meaning as Starting Points. A person may find an interaction absorbing without experiencing the object or activity as particularly significant; likewise, a person may experience an object or activity as meaningful but find little enjoyment in it. We have just seen examples of how an absorbing relationship becomes meaningful. Does the presence of one quality facilitate development of the other quality of a person's relationship to the world? This is an important question because there is some empirical evidence that absorption without felt meaning, and subjective significance without enjoyment, both are experienced by talented young people as inadequate bases for long-term engagement (Csikszentmihalyi, Rathunde, and Whalen, 1993).

There is reason to think that if creative work, service work, or any other relationship to the world is experienced as absorbing, interaction with the object favors the emergence of felt meaning. Likewise, there is some reason to think that if a relationship to the world is subjectively meaningful, a person is more likely to find flow in it. Consider two qualities of a person's interactions with the object that can contribute to this. First, experiencing flow in a relationship and experiencing a relationship as meaningful both motivate *persistent involvement* with the object. Second, both motivate *receptive attention* to the object.

Persistence holds a person in sustained interaction with the object. It thus encourages a flow activity's accrual of meaning through direct experience because connections between person and world accumulate only gradually over the course of a relationship. Persistence also increases the chances of finding flow in a meaningful activity because flow requires a level of skill and may be experienced only after enduring initial frustrations (Allport, 1937; Csikszentmihalyi, 1990). For example, experiencing some sphere (such as social work or journalism) as the solution to an existential problem serves to bring the person into contact with the object. Through the resulting interactions, the individual may discover and develop a set of skills and strengths that make this relationship to the world enjoyably absorbing as well as meaningful. The relationship can evolve into vital engagement.

Keen attention, what Dewey (1934) referred to as perception in contrast to recognition, fosters the emergence of both absorption and meaning. The attentiveness inspired by flow or by felt meaning entails an attitude of openness, or receptivity, in the course of experience with the object, rather than the mere registering of experience. This heightened receptivity encourages people to observe a role model, take in the unintended consequences of their actions, learn from social influences (Colby and Damon, 1992), and adjust their goals and meaning systems based on interactions with the world. In summary, many factors might contribute to finding either absorption or meaning in interactions with the world. Further, each favors the development of a more complex relationship to the world, one of vital engagement.

Conclusion

This chapter has drawn on the accounts of adults who are deeply engaged with the work that they do. It is intended to provide a conceptual tool to those studying and encouraging engagement in youth. Family members, mentors, and more distant influences are often important precisely because observing or working with them enables young people to envision their own future in terms of vital engagement. The study of engaged adults likewise helps to identify possibilities for adulthood toward which young people might seek to move, by showing how vital engagement with some aspect of the world can become an organizing principle in a person's life.

Vital engagement lies at the intersection of immediate experience and the life course. It is distinguished by deeply absorbing interactions; these experiences of absorption, or flow, are embedded in an enduring relationship. Engagement connects the individual to something beyond the self. The examples in this chapter were drawn from creative work and service work. These particular self-object relationships merit special attention because they have the capacity to significantly transform culture and society. However, any sphere of life can be vitally engaging.

All such relationships transform both the object and the individual. For the individual, valued aspects of the self find expression and realization in the relationship to the object. In addition, vital engagement contributes to a person's overall well-being. Happiness and a sense that life has meaning are attained not by directly pursuing them but as by-products of being vitally engaged with the world.

References

Abelove, H., and others (eds.). *Visions of History*. New York: Pantheon Books, 1983.
Allport, G. *Pattern and Growth in Personality*. Austin, Tex.: Holt, Rinehart and Winston, 1937.
Andrews, M. *Lifetimes of Commitment*. Cambridge: Cambridge University Press, 1991.
Berger, P., and Luckmann, T. *The Social Construction of Reality*. New York: Doubleday, 1966.
Bloom, B. S. (ed.). *Developing Talent in Young People*. New York: Ballantine Books, 1985.
Carlson, R. "Studies in Script Theory." *Perceptual and Motor Skills*, 1982, *55*, 595–610.
Cohler, B. J. "Personal Narrative and the Life Course." In P. B. Baltes and O. G. Brim (eds.), *Life-Span Development and Behavior*. Vol. 4. New York: Academic Press, 1982.
Colby, A., and Damon, W. *Some Do Care: Contemporary Lives of Moral Commitment*. New York: Free Press, 1992.
Csikszentmihalyi, M. *Beyond Boredom and Anxiety*. San Francisco: Jossey-Bass, 1975.
Csikszentmihalyi, M. *Flow: The Psychology of Optimal Experience*. New York: HarperCollins, 1990.
Csikszentmihalyi, M. *Creativity: Flow and the Psychology of Discovery and Invention*. New York: HarperCollins, 1996.
Csikszentmihalyi, M. *Finding Flow: The Psychology of Engagement with Everyday Life*. New York: Basic Books, 1997.
Csikszentmihalyi, M., and Beattie, O. "Life Themes: A Theoretical and Empirical Exploration of Their Origins and Effects." *Journal of Humanistic Psychology*, 1979, *19*, 45–63.
Csikszentmihalyi, M., and Csikszentmihalyi, I. S. (eds.). *Optimal Experience: Psychological Studies of Flow in Consciousness*. New York: Cambridge University Press, 1988.
Csikszentmihalyi, M., and Nakamura, J. "Emerging Goals and the Self-Regulation of Behavior." In R. S. Wyer (ed.), *Advances in Social Cognition, Vol. 12: Perspectives on Behavioral Self-Regulation*. Mahwah, N.J.: Erlbaum, 1999.
Csikszentmihalyi, M., and Rathunde, K. "The Development of the Person: An Experiential Perspective on the Ontogenesis of Psychological Complexity." In R. M. Lerner (ed.), *Handbook of Child Psychology. Vol. 1: Theoretical Models of Human Development*. New York: Wiley, 1998.
Csikszentmihalyi, M., Rathunde, K., and Whalen, S. *Talented Teenagers: The Roots of Success and Failure*. New York: Cambridge University Press, 1993.
Csikszentmihalyi, M., and Robinson, R. *The Art of Seeing*. Malibu, Calif.: Getty Trust, 1990.
Csikszentmihalyi, M., and Rochberg-Halton, E. *The Meaning of Things*. New York: Cambridge University Press, 1981.
Daloz, L., Keen, C., Keen, J., and Parks, S. *Common Fire*. Boston: Beacon Press, 1996.
Dewey, J. *How We Think*. Lexington, Mass.: Heath, 1910.
Dewey, J. *Interest and Effort in Education*. Cambridge, Mass.: Riverside Press, 1913.
Dewey, J. *Human Nature and Conduct*. New York: Random House, 1930.
Dewey, J. *Art as Experience*. New York: Capricorn Books, 1934.
Dewey, J. *Experience and Education*. New York: Collier Books, 1938.
Fink, B. "Interest Development as Structural Change in Person-Object Relationships." In L. Oppenheimer and J. Valsiner (eds.), *The Origins of Action: Interdisciplinary and International Perspectives*. New York: Springer-Verlag, 1991.
Inghilleri, P. *From Subjective Experience to Cultural Change*. New York: Cambridge University Press, 1999.
Jackson, P. *John Dewey and the Lessons of Art*. New Haven, Conn.: Yale University Press, 1998.
James, W. *The Principles of Psychology*. Cambridge, Mass.: Harvard University Press, 1981. (Originally published 1890.)
Magnusson, D., and Stattin, H. "Person-Context Interaction Theories." In R. M. Lerner (ed.), *Handbook of Child Psychology. Vol. 1: Theoretical Models of Human Development*. New York: Wiley, 1998.

Massimini, F., and Delle Fave, A. "Individual Development in a Bio-Cultural Perspective." *American Psychologist,* 2000, *55,* 24–33.
McAdams, D. *Stories We Live By.* New York: Morrow, 1993.
Mead, G. H. *Mind, Self and Society.* Chicago: University of Chicago Press, 1934.
Neugarten, B. "Continuities and Discontinuities of Psychological Issues into Adult Life." *Human Development,* 1969, *12,* 121–130.
Ochse, R. *Before the Gates of Excellence.* Cambridge: Cambridge University Press, 1990.
Rathunde, K. "Wisdom and Abiding Interest: Interviews with Three Noted Historians in Later-Life." *Journal of Adult Development,* 1995, *2,* 159–172.
Renninger, K., Hidi, S., and Krapp, A. (eds.). *The Role of Interest in Learning and Development.* Mahwah, N.J.: Erlbaum, 1992.
Renninger, K., and Leckrone, T. "Continuity in Young Children's Actions: A Consideration of Interest and Temperament." In L. Oppenheimer and J. Valsiner (eds.), *The Origins of Action: Interdisciplinary and International Perspectives.* New York: Springer-Verlag, 1991.
Seligman, M., and Csikszentmihalyi, M. "Positive Psychology: An Introduction." *American Psychologist,* 2000, *55,* 5–14.
Weisskopf-Joelson, E. "Meaning as an Integrating Factor." In C. Buhler and F. Massarik (eds.), *The Course of Human Life.* New York: Springer, 1968.
White, R. W. (ed.). *The Study of Lives: Essays in Honor of Henry A. Murray.* New York: Atherton, 1963.
Yalom, I. D. *Existential Psychotherapy.* New York: Basic Books, 1980.

JEANNE NAKAMURA is research director at the Quality of Life Research Center, Claremont Graduate University.

2

Academically and artistically talented youngsters have been well studied, but little focus has been directed to understanding young activists. This chapter considers what elements might contribute to a clear pattern of moral action in a young person who is "morally gifted."

A Model of Extraordinary Social Engagement, or "Moral Giftedness"

Mimi Michaelson

Mother Teresa, Florence Nightingale, and Mahatma Gandhi, individuals we see as moral icons, are said to have demonstrated unusual moral concerns early on (Boss, 1994; Gardner, 1993). Today there are children as young as nine who are not only making sense of what is right and wrong but also taking concrete steps to redress inequities or contribute to social causes. Consider two cases of extraordinary social engagement, or what I shall call "moral giftedness."

While working on an article for a children's radio show, nine-year-old Emily Kumpel first learned that book shortages in apartheid South Africa were impeding access to education for black children. Soliciting help from others, Emily led a drive to send books to South Africa. Thus far, Emily has collected over two million textbooks for South African students (Burge, 1998; Kumpel, personal communication, 2000).

When he was twelve, Craig Kielburger read about the murder of a child who had been sold into bondage in a carpet factory in Pakistan. Moved by the plight of this child, Craig recruited family and friends to launch a campaign to fight child labor. Eventually Craig founded Free the Children, an international organization that combats child exploitation. Thus far, Craig has traveled to over thirty countries to spread his message and has been internationally recognized by awards including the Global

This work was made possible by the generous support of the Louise and Claude Rosenberg Jr. Family Foundation. I wish to thank the three principal investigators of the Good Work Project, Mihaly Csikszentmihalyi, William Damon, and Howard Gardner, for their continued support. I also wish to thank the members of the Harvard research team.

Leader of Tomorrow award at the World Economic Forum in Davos, Switzerland (Kielburger, 1998).

Academically and artistically talented youngsters have been well studied, but little focus has been directed to understanding young activists. Emily, Craig, and others are readily identifiable as young activists and excel in the moral dimension. Such "morally gifted" youth, unusually committed to community service and social action, are identified globally through awards like the Reebok Human Rights Youth-in-Action Awards and locally by schools or newspapers. Some of these young people exhibit strong leadership abilities, whereas in others the desire to help persons in need is most evident. Looking at these cases enables us to ask the following questions: What are the elements of moral giftedness, or extraordinary social engagement, in youth? What qualities contribute to a clear pattern of moral action in a young person?

Scope of This Chapter

I begin by defining giftedness and morality and then propose a framework of moral action. I apply this framework to two relevant bodies of literature, and I focus on the question of what elements might contribute to moral giftedness. This literature includes empirical studies of the gifted that touch on moral abilities and empirical studies of moral exemplars, including current adolescent social activists and retrospective accounts of adult activists (such as civil rights activists or those who rescued Holocaust victims). As I do not intend to claim that young moral exemplars necessarily turn into adult moral exemplars (for instance, that a young moral Gandhi becomes an adult moral exemplar), I use the retrospective accounts only as background.

Definitions

I begin with studies of the traditionally gifted because these identify a range of unusual moral abilities. By *traditionally gifted* I mean children performing at a high level in any one recognized societal domain (Feldman and Goldsmith, 1986). *Talent* and *giftedness,* terms that I use interchangeably, often refer to children who excel in academic pursuits. However, these terms are also applied to the arts, athletics, or other domains and could, I suggest, be invoked with reference to moral behavior.

My definition of *morality* incorporates features of reasoning and behavior but highlights action. In particular, I construe morality as including a consideration of, and an obligation to act on the basis of, others' needs and as encompassing action in accordance with a socially acceptable set of codes with consideration of the rights of others (Damon, 1988). I assume that all children have some moral sense but am particularly interested in those who demonstrate extraordinary action—those who might be morally gifted. I use the term *morally gifted* to highlight a possible end state of unusual moral commitment that would be manifested in service or action exemplifying the highest degree of social engagement.

Morally gifted children, socially engaged youth, and *young moral actors* are terms that I use interchangeably and that include children and adolescents who demonstrate unusual, far-reaching, and independent voluntary action for another's benefit (Eisenberg and Mussen, 1989). By *independent* I mean actions that are individually initiated (for example, starting a book campaign rather than participating in an already existing drive). By *far-reaching* I mean actions directed beyond the immediate or personal toward a larger, more distant goal. Rather than being directed at helping a specific situation or individual, these actions are aimed at a wider canvas. Such actions have the potential to affect many people as well as to create long-term change (for example, by the creation of an institution). Examples include organizing a local homeless shelter or a book drive for children in South Africa, as opposed to an individual act of kindness, like giving a book to a homeless child.

Although individual voluntary acts may be necessary developmental precursors, it is the larger-scale acts that I highlight. I am interested in actions of wider scope for several reasons: although there are anecdotal accounts of unusual young moral actors, there is little or no systematic study of this kind of broad-sweeping activism; and although, by definition, the study of unusual talent is not generalizable to the everyday, it does help us better understand the whole array of abilities in a particular domain. In this case we might better understand the range of abilities related to extraordinary social engagement or even moral leadership.

A Framework for Examining the Literature

How one acts morally is a complex phenomenon. I believe that at least three components are critical for unusual and far-reaching independent voluntary actions:

- The *perception* of a situation as being appropriate for moral consideration
- The *reflection* on the meaning of this situation and one's personal relation to it, including evaluating potential personal actions or decisions about what is the "right" course of action
- The assumption of personal responsibility, or *action,* in response to a situation regardless of the consequences

These different aspects of moral action may rely on different abilities. I will review what we know about related "moral abilities" and place them within the framework of perception, reflection, and action. My goal in reviewing this literature is to build a hypothetical portrait of a young moral exemplar.

I begin by looking at some traits noted in the traditionally gifted. (For related frameworks see Gardner, 1989; Tishman, 1995.)

Current Research on the Traditionally Gifted

Empirical studies of the traditionally gifted report a range of unusual moral abilities, often described as "moral sensitivity" (Silverman, 1994). According to Silverman, "We have dozens of cases on record of gifted children fighting injustice, befriending and protecting handicapped children, conserving resources, responding to other's emotional needs, becoming terribly upset if a classmate is humiliated . . . writing letters to the President to try and end the Gulf War, and writing poems of anguish at the cruelty in the world" (p. 111). These sensitivities take many forms, including empathy, social and political awareness, perspective taking, and moral reasoning. These components are considered by some as fundamental to giftedness. Using the framework of moral action lets us parse "moral sensitivities" into different components; empathy and social and political awareness might add to our perception of moral issues, and perspective taking and moral reasoning might aid our reflection on these issues. I will explain why each ability may be primarily situated in a given category. Of course, different moral abilities may not always fit neatly into one compartment.

The Way Gifted Children Perceive Situations

What does literature on the gifted say about how children perceive a situation?

Empathy. Children of high intellectual ability are sometimes described as more aware of emotional cues, or more empathic, recognizing another child's hurt feelings or responding to someone in need (Silverman, 1994). Two elements of this emotional response include felt experience and perception of another's feelings (Mendaglio, 1995). The first suggests that gifted children experience emotions at a deeper level than peers. This is also sometimes described as "overexcitability" or "intensity" (Kitano, 1990). The second emotional element, a greater sensitivity to the feelings of others, is influenced by the first. For example, Roeper (1982) describes the emotional awareness of a gifted child involved in a chess match. She offers an example of a winning child who loses interest in the match when he notices his opponent's emotional distress. This child is described as being unusually cognizant of another child's feelings. When referring to the emotional sensitivity of the gifted, Lovecky (1992, p. 21) describes "a depth of feeling that results in a sense of identification with others (people, animals, nature, the universe)." In this instance a greater felt experience makes one more aware of the feelings of others and aids perception.

Awareness of Social and Political Issues. Gifted children are also said to read newspapers more often (Clark and Hankins, 1985) and are more aware of and troubled by social and moral issues (Hollingworth, 1942; Winner, 1996). Gifted children describe their concerns with world problems; 80 percent of those interviewed in one study saw themselves as more concerned about global issues than their nongifted peers (Galbraith, 1985; Roeper, 1988).

Although being more informed about the world does not predict how one will behave, broader interest or knowledge might contribute to an increased social radar and help one perceive a situation as morally charged. Social and global awareness are particularly important as a link to far-reaching action because it is difficult to act if one is uninformed.

The Way Gifted Children Reflect on Situations

What does literature on the gifted say about how children reflect on a situation? Perspective taking and moral reasoning are two key factors described in literature on the traditionally gifted. Both influence the way we reflect on the moral implications of any given situation.

Perspective-Taking Ability. Perspective taking centers on the ability to understand someone else's thinking. This is distinct from empathy, which is considered an emotional response. Some research suggests that the intellectually gifted not only have greater self-awareness but also have an enhanced ability to understand the viewpoints of others (Andreani and Pagnin, 1993; Mendaglio, 1995; Rothenberg, 1970). Social perspective taking is said to be associated with giftedness, whereas affective perspective taking is correlated with IQ from as early as preschool (Abroms and Gollin, 1980; Janos and Robinson, 1985).

Cognitive strengths are believed to aid the traditionally gifted in making inferences about how others think. It is possible that the gifted are better at making inferences simply because they have more practice; they are better at noticing the subtleties of interpersonal dialogue and behavior. For example, they are more likely than others to notice facial expressions or tone of voice (Mendaglio, 1995). The tendency to be more observant might help one recognize a situation that inspires moral consideration. Furthermore, the ability to take another's view could help in reflecting on the circumstance, once recognized. In fact, practice in perspective taking (for example, through peer interaction or dialogue) is considered to be essential in the development of moral reasoning and prosocial behavior (Eisenberg and Mussen, 1989; Selman, 1980).

Moral Reasoning. Most of the research that links moral ability to the gifted has focused directly on moral reasoning. Kohlberg (1969), the most widely cited researcher on this subject, advanced the area of study by looking at children's reasoning in response to dilemmas describing six sequential stages, from concrete to abstract understanding.

Using Kohlberg's dilemmas, studies have found a correlation between IQ and level of moral reasoning; those with high IQs reason at a higher level

(Andreani and Pagnin, 1993; Diessner, 1983; Janos and Robinson, 1985). In addition, those with high IQs reach a higher level of moral reasoning earlier than their peers do (Karnes and Brown, 1981; Tan-Willman and Gutteridge, 1981). Fewer than 10 percent of ordinary adults progress beyond the Conventional stages (Winner, 1996). Interestingly, during their teens, some children with high IQs reason at a Principled level, a level attained only by a small subset of adults (Narvaez, 1993; Janos and Robinson, 1985; Winner, 1996). Some authors believe that moral ability rests on reasoning ability and is therefore constrained by level of cognition (Andreani and Pagnin, 1993).

Both a greater ability to take another's view and advanced reasoning could add to one's capacity to reflect on a moral situation. If reasoning develops early or to a greater extent (for example, allowing one to consider abstract principles rather than concrete examples), then it seems likely that one's ability to evaluate the rightness or fairness of a situation might be enhanced.

How one reasons with respect to moral dilemmas may suggest how well one is able to think or reflect about a situation (judgment as a measure of cognitive ability) and how one might act in the real world (judgment as a measure of potential behavior). Whereas the first assumption still has some weight (as seen in its relation to IQ), the second turns out to be more problematic.

Limitations of Research on Gifted Children

A review of research on the gifted highlights several limitations. Most of the work looks at children with above average IQs (often reflected in high academic achievement) and focuses on the cognitive aspects of morality, such as reasoning about moral dilemmas (Andreani and Pagnin, 1993; Silverman, 1994; Winner, 1996). The focus on cognitive ability overlooks other kinds of talent. For example, there is little research on children with musical and moral abilities or physical and moral strengths.

In addition, literature on the gifted tells us little about how gifted children act when confronted with a social problem. When research on the traditionally gifted does tell us about how these abilities are related to action, the claims are restricted. There are two main points to be considered: how empathic feelings motivate actions and how higher cognitive abilities are indicative of a coherence of values and action.

Do Empathic Feelings Motivate Action? Writing about the morally sensitive, Lovecky (1992, p. 21) suggests that those who are empathic are also moved to act: "Compassion refers to the sense of caring many gifted children show for others, enabling them to make commitments to social causes from a desire to decrease the pain they see in others." (See also Silverman, 1994.)

However, these authors do not fully explain how the move from feeling or perception to action occurs. Nor do they explain why in some cases an empathic child might act and in other cases might not. For example, even if a child feels distress at the plight of others, the child still may not intervene. In fact, it is probable that in most cases she would not intervene. Suggesting that perception automatically implies action does not go far enough.

Do Cognitive Abilities Relate to Action? The second point has to do with how cognitive ability may be related to action. The traditionally gifted are said to have a greater need to align their personal values with their behavior (Clark, 1983). The connection between values and behavior is supported by other research that notes that those who reason at a higher level are more likely to be concerned with how their actions reflect their beliefs (Blasi, 1980; Haan, Smith, and Block, 1968; Rothman, 1992). However, these studies highlight different points. For example, some studies indicate that higher reasoning is related to honesty or altruism (Blasi, 1980), whereas others imply that those with higher intelligence and higher reasoning are less likely to conform to the views of others and that their actions reflect this independence (Haan Smith, and Block, 1968). In addition, studies about higher reasoning do not specifically refer to gifted children. Although such claims are certainly of interest, the use of different definitions, populations, and theoretical assumptions make the claims difficult to compare. Yet even if traditionally gifted students may be more aware of social issues, better able to reflect on them, or more concerned with how to integrate beliefs with behavior, questions remain. It is not clear whether this awareness or reflection inspires action or ethical behavior when individuals are confronted with real-life situations.

Studies of adult moral exemplars, such as those who rescued Holocaust victims (Oliner and Oliner, 1988), demonstrate that high moral reasoning does not correlate with prosocial behavior (Colby and Damon, 1992). For example, Colby and Damon interviewed a nominated group of twenty-three unusually altruistic adults, including civil rights workers, peace activists, environmentalists, and those who worked with the poor. Half of this group demonstrated reasoning at Kohlberg's Conventional level rather than at the predicted highest Postconventional level. Since that study, there have been similar findings; a study of inner-city adolescents found no difference in moral reasoning between a group of "caring" adolescents and a matched comparison group (Hart and Fegley, 1995).

Literature on the traditionally gifted depicts some moral abilities that are useful in building a portrait of the morally gifted. However, this is only a starting point. Given that we know little about how these gifted children act in the real world, this emerging portrait needs to be supplemented with what we know about those who have a history of activism. For this background I turn to additional literature on activists and moral exemplars.

Research on Activists and Moral Exemplars

Research on real-life exemplars includes studies of inner-city adolescent caregivers (Hart and Fegley, 1995), Peace Corps volunteers (Hoehn, 1983), civil rights activists (McAdam, 1988; Coles and Brenner, 1965;

Rosenhan, 1970), Holocaust rescuers (London, 1970; Oliner and Oliner, 1988), and individuals who demonstrate a lifetime of committed action (Colby and Damon, 1992). Looking at those with a history of activism allows us to work backward and note features in real-life exemplars that could explain unusual moral actions.

Although research on real-life exemplars covers a broad spectrum of situations and actions, shared features do appear across these different groups: social and political awareness, centrality of relationships, coherence of goals, and optimism. These features can also be looked at within the framework of the three-pronged model of moral action described earlier (perception, reflection, and action). Greater awareness of social and political issues and centrality of relationships are more closely related to how we perceive a situation; the remaining characteristics primarily shed light on the final aspect of the model—how we act.

Perception. What does literature on moral exemplars say about the way they perceive a situation?

Social and Political Awareness. Research tells us that activists are generally more aware of social and political issues than nonactivists and that they may acquire this awareness at an earlier age (Oliner and Oliner, 1988). Perception of issues as deserving of moral consideration may also be related to knowing about the larger world.

It makes sense intuitively that knowledge of issues would encourage perception of an issue as morally relevant. However, additional developmental factors may also play a role in the acquisition of political awareness. For example, comparing nonactivists with activist adolescents, Merelman and King (1986) found that the young activists had a more developed ideological framework than the nonactivists. This ideological framework is used to organize considerations of social and political issues. Hence, how this information is structured may also be critical and linked to some aspect of cognitive development. Understanding the cognitive abilities that underlie these frameworks and guide the interpretation of events may inform our understanding of a developmental baseline.

Centrality of Relationships. Empirical work on activists suggests a profile of individuals who recognize the importance of close relationships (London, 1970; Oliner and Oliner, 1988; Rosenhan, 1970). Those who rescued Jews from the Nazis are described as embedded in a network of relationships that include close ties with family and friends. In their study of those who rescued Jews from the Nazis, Oliner and Oliner outline their findings this way: "[P]arents set high standards for their children to meet, particularly with regard to caring for others. Because of their solid family relationships, such children tend to internalize their parents' values, increasingly incorporating standards for personal integrity and care within their own value systems" (p. 250).

A history of caring relationships may prompt perception by contributing to one's ability to consider how an issue is personally relevant. According to Gilligan (1982), these individuals may demonstrate an ethic of caring; people in caring relationships are more likely to help others. These salient early experiences may get extended from the personal to the public; in other words, those who learn to care and respect those close by may be more inclined to care about those who are more remote.

Action. What does literature on moral exemplars say about moral action? Now we turn to considering some of the factors mentioned in the research on activists and moral exemplars that may better explain why individuals might act. These include efficacy, confidence in action, social awareness, and faith. Two major factors, which will be considered here, are coherence of goals and optimism.

Coherence of Goals. Moral exemplars who demonstrate sustained moral commitment exhibit unity of their identity and morality. This is described by Colby and Damon (1992) as a coherence of personal and moral goals. These altruistic adults describe their social commitments as integral to their views of themselves. Although outsiders might see these exemplars' actions as heroic, the exemplars themselves have so integrated the notion of morality into their views of themselves that they recount their actions as everyday events.

Colby and Damon's observations (1992) are supported by research on the self-concept of prosocial inner-city adolescents (Hart and Fegley, 1995). Hart and Fegley believe that moral commitment can best be understood by seeing how individuals view themselves. Their research on prosocial adolescents indicates that when the individual's notion of an ideal self (what I hope to be) and actual self (what I am) overlap—in other words, when personal and moral goals are united—action on the basis of these moral values is more straightforward.

Personifying this personal stake and urge to act, a civil rights activist remarks, "I couldn't shake off the notion that suffering hurts and that I'm in a position to alleviate it sometimes. I have seen suffering, and just because I would prefer not to be bothered by it, that doesn't take away my responsibilities. It doesn't take away my consciousness. I can't just say, 'Well to hell with suffering, I've done my share'" (Hoehn, 1983, p. 25). In this example the moral becomes personal as the subject realizes her own responsibility and her relationship to another's suffering.

Moral exemplars are also said to act without hesitation and with great certainty, often under difficult circumstances. This does not mean that risks go unrecognized; rather, problems are not allowed to deter the "necessary" action. These findings resonate with the work of others who note that moral exemplars talk about their heroic actions as obvious and devoid of choice (Hoehn, 1983; McAdam, 1988; Oliner and Oliner, 1988).

Those with greater moral coherence might be more likely to act on another's behalf to avoid or reduce internal conflict. One acts because inaction conflicts with self-understanding.

Optimism. Many adult activists are also described as optimistic (Colby and Damon, 1992). How do activists persist when some problems are monumental? There are several mechanisms that may help. One way of coping is by reframing and diminishing the importance of setbacks. Exemplars may do this by attributing defeats to external events; for example, they may view a situation as unusual or of limited duration rather than as the result of a personal quality. How one explains uncontrollable events is said to determine how helpless or energized a person feels in response to trying situations (Seligman, 1995). Optimists are more likely to see causes as external and bounded (as opposed to internal and pervasive) and can therefore temper their response to challenging circumstances. Hence an optimist is more likely to feel empowered than disabled by challenge. Moral exemplars often embody this kind of optimistic reframing.

Limitations of Research on Activists and Moral Exemplars

Research on moral exemplars also has its limitations. One important issue is that many of the studies, including those of Holocaust rescuers, rely on retrospective accounts. With the frailty of memory and hindsight there is potential for altered histories—for example, changed recollections of how parents modeled behavior or how promptly one reacted in a situation. For more reliable data additional research is needed to supplement these retrospective findings.

In addition, there are obvious problems in comparing traits across quite disparate circumstances. Comparing findings about a Holocaust rescuer to studies involving an inner-city adolescent volunteer overlooks the very different contexts of those activities. For example, did the action put the subject at risk? Was this action unique or part of a lifelong pattern? These kinds of differences illustrate the complexity of actions and the motivations that prompt them.

Finally, there is little empirical research on contemporary young activists and on unusual moral abilities of children. Most research on moral development and children has focused on moral reasoning or on laboratory studies of altruism. These studies are of marginal utility in explaining real-life behavior; they are sometimes overly contrived (for example, studies of how children compete for an item), often focused on limited populations, and frequently too far removed from actual experiences to fully mirror the complexities of daily life.

Summary of What We Know About Activists and Moral Exemplars

Literature on activists and moral exemplars adds to what we know about "moral ability" by revealing certain factors associated with how individuals act in the real world or become socially engaged. Activists and moral exemplars are said to be more socially and politically aware and more supported by close relationships. These features contribute primarily to one's ability to perceive an issue as within the moral sphere. For instance, those who learn to care or who are more socially aware might be more likely to recognize moral issues in the first place.

Of course, these factors alone are not sufficient to explain how individuals act in unusual, far-reaching, and independent ways. Additional qualities contribute to the action element of the proposed framework. Two of these action-oriented elements are optimism and coherence of goals. These features go beyond explaining how individuals may become more aware of moral issues, or how they reflect on them, to consider the psychological reasons and motivations that prompt a response.

Emerging Profile of the Young Moral Actor

Based on what we know about exemplary moral actors and those who are traditionally gifted with "moral abilities," we can begin to build a preliminary profile of a young moral actor. Consider a young moral actor named Janice. After viewing a television news program about Rwandan refugees, Janice decides to launch a campaign to send books to children in Rwandan refugee camps. What traits might we see in Janice?

Based on a review of some literature, we can speculate about a possible collection of traits. Perhaps Janice is empathic and feels strongly about the feelings of others. These feelings of care may get extended beyond her immediate sphere to those who are more remote. We expect that Janice is personally invested in her book campaign, though she may not articulate sophisticated moral principles. As we look more closely at Janice's background, we might see other relevant factors. For example, Janice might come from a close and socially aware family. Perhaps she is influenced by her parents and is therefore more aware of social and political issues than her peers are. We might also see that Janice is self-motivated and that her actions reflect her belief that how she acts is critical to who she is.

Conclusion

The foregoing profile is made up of traits culled from the two bodies of relevant literature examined: empirical studies of the gifted that touch on moral abilities and empirical studies on activists and moral exemplars. These are only some of the traits one might expect to see in a young activist. If there is a kind of moral giftedness, or unusual social engagement, it would take on different forms and vary according to a host of factors. Although some traits may appear in one instance, we would not expect to see all in any one individual.

The question remains about what we would find in an empirical study of exemplary young moral actors, or those who might be morally gifted. In other words, rather than simply considering what traits appear in Janice, in ongoing work I am considering what traits appear in ten subjects like Janice.

In this research, the following questions might arise: Do young moral actors show unusual empathy? Do they show greater skill in moral reasoning or other cognitive abilities? Other questions appear as we consider what factors motivate adult activists. For example, do young activists describe caring families? Are they optimistic or quick to act? And finally, are additional traits apparent?

These are only some of the questions that naturally surface. This chapter proposes a preliminary framework for understanding unusual moral action and an initial set of questions to explore. In an age when headlines almost daily describe youth tragedy, it seems particularly pressing to highlight the best of what young people have to offer. Through their contributions and commitments, young activists give us a glimpse of this potential.

References

Abroms, K. I., and Gollin, J. B. "Developmental Study of Gifted Preschool Children and Measures of Psychosocial Giftedness." *Exceptional Children,* 1980, *46,* 334–341.

Andreani, O. D., and Pagnin, A. "Nurturing the Moral Development of the Gifted." In K. A. Heller, F. J. Monks, and A. H. Passow (eds.), *International Handbook of Research and Development of Giftedness and Talent.* New York: Pergamon Press, 1993.

Blasi, A. "Bridging Moral Cognition and Moral Action: A Critical Review of the Literature." *Psychological Bulletin,* 1980, *88,* 1–45.

Boss, J. "The Autonomy of Moral Intelligence." *Educational Theory,* 1994, *44,* 399–415.

Burge, K. "Prodigies." *Attaché,* Apr. 1998, pp. 80–87.

Clark, B. *Growing up Gifted: Developing the Potential of Children at Home and at School.* (2nd ed.) Columbus, Ohio: Charles E. Merrill, 1983.

Clark, W. H., and Hankins, N. E. "Giftedness and Conflict." *Roeper Review,* 1985, *8,* 50–53.

Colby, A., and Damon, W. *Some Do Care: Contemporary Lives of Moral Commitment.* New York: Free Press, 1992.

Coles, R., and Brenner, J. "American Youth in a Social Struggle: The Mississippi Summer Project." *American Journal of Orthopsychiatry,* 1965, *35,* 909–926.

Damon, W. *The Moral Child.* New York: Free Press, 1988.

Diessner, R. "The Relationship Between Cognitive Abilities and Moral Development in Intellectually Gifted Children." *Gifted Child Today,* 1983, *28,* 15–17.

Eisenberg, N., and Mussen, P. H. *The Roots of Prosocial Behavior in Children.* New York: Cambridge University Press, 1989.

Feldman, D., and Goldsmith, L. *Nature's Gambit.* New York: Basic Books, 1986.

Galbraith, J. "The Eight Great Gripes of Gifted Kids: Responding to Special Needs." *Roeper Review,* 1985, *8,* 15–18.

Gardner, H. "Zero-Based Arts Education: An Introduction to Arts PROPEL." *Studies in Art Education: A Journal of Issues and Research,* 1989, *30,* 71–83.

Gardner, H. *Creating Minds.* New York: Basic Books, 1993.

Gilligan, C. *In a Different Voice.* Cambridge, Mass.: Harvard University Press, 1982.

Haan, N., Smith, M. B., and Block, J. "Moral Reasoning of Young Adults: Political-Social Behavior, Family Background, and Personality Correlates." *Journal of Personality and Social Psychology,* 1968, *10,* 183–201.

Hart, D., and Fegley, S. "Prosocial Behavior and Caring in Adolescence: Relations to Self-Understanding and Social Judgment." *Child Development,* 1995, *66,* 1346–1359.

Hoehn, R. A. *Up from Apathy.* Nashville, Tenn.: Abingdon Press, 1983.

Hollingworth, L. S. *Children Above 180 IQ: Origin and Development.* New York: World Book, 1942.

Janos, P. M., and Robinson, N. M. "Psychosocial Development in Intellectually Gifted Children." In F. D. Horowitz and M. O'Brien (eds.), *The Gifted and Talented: Developmental Perspectives.* Washington, D.C.: American Psychological Association, 1985.

Karnes, F., and Brown, K. E. "Moral Development and the Gifted." *Roeper Review,* 1981, *3,* 8–10.

Kielburger, C. *Free the Children.* New York: HarperCollins, 1998.

Kitano, M. K. "Intellectual Abilities and Psychological Intensities in Young Children: Implications for the Gifted." *Roeper Review,* 1990, *13,* 5–10.

Kohlberg, L. "Stage and Sequence: The Cognitive-Developmental Approach to Socialization." In D. A. Goslin (ed.), *Handbook of Socialization Theory and Research.* Skokie, Ill.: Rand McNally, 1969.

London, P. "The Rescuers: Motivational Hypotheses About Christians Who Saved Jews from the Nazis." In J. Macaulay and L. Berkowitz (eds.), *Altruism and Helping Behavior: Social Psychological Studies of Some Antecedents and Consequences.* New York: Academic Press, 1970.

Lovecky, D. V. "Exploring Social and Emotional Aspects of Giftedness." *Roeper Review,* 1992, *15,* 18–25.

McAdam, D. *Freedom Summer.* New York: Oxford University Press, 1988.

Mendaglio, S. "Sensitivity Among Gifted Persons: A Multi-Faceted Perspective." *Roeper Review,* 1995, *17,* 169–172.

Merelman, R. M., and King, G. "The Development of Political Activists: Toward a Model of Early Learning." *Social Science Quarterly,* 1986, *67,* 473–490.

Narvaez, D. "High Achieving Students and Moral Judgment." *Journal for the Education of the Gifted,* 1993, *16,* 268–279.

Oliner, S. P., and Oliner, P. M. *The Altruistic Personality: Rescuers of Jews in Nazi Europe.* New York: Free Press, 1988.

Roeper, A. "How the Gifted Cope with Their Emotions." *Roeper Review,* 1982, *11,* 21–24.

Roeper, A. "Should Educators of the Gifted and Talented Be More Concerned with World Issues?" *Roeper Review,* 1988, *11,* 12–13.

Rosenhan, D. "The Natural Socialization of Altruistic Autonomy." In J. Macaulay and L. Berkowitz (eds.), *Altruism and Helping Behavior: Social Psychological Studies of Some Antecedents and Consequences.* New York: Academic Press, 1970.

Rothenberg, B. B. "Children's Social Sensitivity and the Relationship to Interpersonal Competence, Intrapersonal Comfort, and Intellectual Level." *Developmental Psychology,* 1970, *2,* 335–350.

Rothman, G. R. "Moral Reasoning, Moral Behavior, and Moral Giftedness: A Developmental Perspective." In P. S. Klein and A. J. Tannenbaum (eds.), *To Be Young and Gifted.* Norwood, N.J.: Ablex, 1992.

Seligman, M. *The Optimistic Child.* Boston: Houghton Mifflin, 1995.

Selman, R. *The Growth of Interpersonal Understanding.* New York: Academic Press, 1980.

Silverman, L. K. "The Moral Sensitivity of Gifted Children and the Evolution of Society." *Roeper Review,* 1994, *17,* 110–116.

Tan-Willman, C., and Gutteridge, D. "Creative Thinking and Moral Reasoning in Academically Gifted Secondary-School Adolescents." *Gifted Child Quarterly,* 1981, *25,* 149–153.

Tishman, S. "The Concept of Intellectual Character and Its Connection to Moral Character." Paper presented at the annual meeting of the American Educational Research Association, San Francisco, Apr. 1995.

Winner, E. *Gifted Children: Myths and Realities.* New York: Basic Books, 1996.

MIMI MICHAELSON is currently a doctoral student at Harvard University and was the senior project manager for the Good Work Project at Harvard.

3

The authors examine factors that motivate and sustain young professionals' commitment to those in need and discuss how individuals come to see service as their life's mission.

The Development of an Enduring Commitment to Service Work

Wendy Fischman, Deborah A. Schutte, Becca Solomon, Grace Wu Lam

> The other night in York Town, I was walking down the street and a homeless man who I'd worked with at the respite program . . . looked up at me and said, "Hello, Beth!" [A]nd I think it was maybe a year since I'd seen him and five years since I'd worked with him as a nurse. But the connections that you make with people and the needs that you're able to help them with . . . being able to meet that kind of need for another human being meets a need for me.

Most of us have a deeper commitment and sense of responsibility to our intimates—family, friends, and colleagues—than to someone whom we have just met. Although perhaps this is a natural response, this situation leaves many less fortunate members of society disenfranchised and without advocates. Luckily, there are some extraordinary people like Beth, the woman quoted at the beginning of this chapter, who are particularly attuned to identifying and caring for those in need, whether or not they know them personally. These are people who cannot walk past a homeless person in the street without worrying. Giving a few dollars—the first reaction many of us

This research was made possible by the generous support of the Louise and Claude Rosenberg Jr. Family Foundation. We thank Principal Investigator Howard Gardner, as well as Jenna Moskowitz and Mimi Michaelson. We also thank Honorable Mark L. Wolf, Lachlan Forrow, Kari Hannibal, and the Schweitzer fellows.

might have—does not suffice; these caring individuals feel the need to involve themselves in profound ways, regardless of what is at stake personally or professionally. What does it take for an individual to connect so deeply to those in need? How does one develop this commitment to service work?

Through studying individuals who are dedicated to community service, we explore what motivates and sustains a deep sense of commitment to those in need. By investigating key elements in their lives—formative experiences, religious beliefs, training opportunities, and mentor relationships—we identify a trajectory of how individuals come to consider service as integral to their life's work. In this chapter we focus on young professionals (in the last stages of graduate training or early job experiences) involved in the Albert Schweitzer Fellowship program. This program provides opportunities for graduate students in health and social services to work in local communities around the United States in addition to the Albert Schweitzer Hospital in West Central Africa. Once fellows are selected to implement their own community-based project, they receive a stipend to carry out the work. Fellows also meet monthly to discuss their project work—the obstacles they encounter and strategies for negotiating these challenges.

Importantly, the focus of this study[1] is on individuals who are deeply committed to service work—those who prioritize helping others as foremost in their lives. In this case the health and social service professionals we studied seek out community involvement and ways to join traditional practice with local needs. The Schweitzer fellows exemplify how their dedication to service work becomes infused in every aspect of their lives, including professional work. Many, if not all, health and social service workers serve others by the nature of their profession, but unlike most, the individuals we interviewed understand service work as their calling. This calling is the principal motivation for entering the profession. In other words, they chose a career that at its core is about helping others because they see their professional work as one avenue toward fulfilling their life's goal.

Background

Literature on the career motivations of health and social service professionals indicates that the desire to help others is a major reason many people, like the Schweitzer fellows, enter these fields. In addition, the scientific nature of the work, intellectual challenge of the career, and high occupational prestige are strong motivations for these professionals (Kutner and Brogan, 1980). Interestingly, in a study of thirty medical students, first-year students were more concerned about "relief of suffering" than fifth-year students, who were more concerned with "material success" (Powell, Boakes, and Slater, 1987). This finding is particularly relevant to our examination of how certain individuals, such as the Schweitzer fellows, develop and maintain an enduring commitment to service.

Previous research also reveals factors that engage and sustain individuals in service work. Role models are common threads in literature on what motivates and sustains service work. First, family and peers are most often identified as sources of inspiration for young people to get involved in community work, especially those engaged in service work themselves (Youniss and Yates, 1997). Parents in particular demonstrate to their children a commitment to caring for others. These parents encourage their children not only to help others but to take responsibility for those in need (Solomon, Watson, and Battistich, forthcoming). Through their example of treating their own children and others around them with compassion and respect, parents may also influence their children to form similar moral goals at an early age (Damon, 1995).

Community service programs hosted by schools and religious organizations also stimulate students to become involved in service work. These early experiences help to shape students' views about themselves, as well as about those they serve. By working closely with people in need, such as the homeless or elderly, young people develop both a sense of responsibility and a sense of agency—a belief that they can make a difference in society. Through their interactions with these individuals, students gain new knowledge of and perspectives on these people. These new understandings and perceptions inspire some young people to want to continue their commitment to service work in the future (Youniss and Yates, 1997; Solomon, Watson, and Battistich, forthcoming).

Some of the influences motivating children's and adolescents' initial involvement in community work, however, have less happy origins. For instance, personal hardships—negative experiences suffered by individuals early on in their lives—are cited as an impetus for adolescents: they want to help those who suffer as they have suffered (Colby and Damon, 1992). The "positivity"—an ability to find hope and joy in everything—that Colby and Damon observed among the moral exemplars they studied is one way these individuals may be distinguished from others who suffer from personal hardship but are not motivated to alleviate the suffering of others. In other words, during difficult times, these individuals may have a sense of optimism, that something good, such as their commitment to service work, can emerge from a painful situation. In numerous cases these optimistic feelings are based on spiritual faith and religious values. This method of "reframing" challenges is a common quality of highly creative individuals (Gardner, 1997). These previous studies not only help us to understand the beginning stages of service work, but they set the context for our research findings about how individuals develop and sustain a commitment to serving others.

This Study

This chapter reports findings from the origins of the Good Work Project. Next we briefly describe the research methodology.

Participants. We interviewed two groups of Schweitzer fellows in the Greater Boston area: eight current fellows (age twenty to thirty) who were nominated by Schweitzer staff and who were engaged in their projects at the time of the interviews and eight former fellows (age twenty-six to thirty-six) who were selected based on final project reports and Schweitzer staff recommendations. Our sample, which consisted of eight women and eight men, included four Asian Americans, one African American, and eleven Caucasians. Their projects ranged from establishing nursing care for homeless people with HIV to working with the homebound elderly.

Method. We conducted an in-depth semistructured interview with each subject. Immediately following each interview, researchers wrote a narrative of the conversation. Interviews were also audiotaped and transcribed for analysis. Researchers developed a coding scheme, based in part on salient themes from the narratives, to examine trends more systematically. Cohen's kappa (1960) was used to calculate interrater agreement ($K = .787$).

A Trajectory of Enduring Commitment

In our study of young professionals dedicated to service work, we learned about their childhood experiences, their personal and professional goals, and their beliefs and values. From sixteen individuals we heard sixteen different stories, yet similar trends emerged with regard to their commitment to service work over time. From these trends, we identified two stages in the trajectory: initial commitment and sustained commitment.

Initial Commitment. These young professionals often traced their commitment to community service back to childhood. Many described hardships they endured early on that propelled them to view service work as an integral component of their lives. Difficult childhood experiences prompted these individuals to develop and recast their life perspectives to include a commitment to helping others suffering similar plights. All but one of the young professionals described their childhood as shaped by one or more of the following: being an outcast, experiencing the death of a parent or close friend, or living with a troubled family member. However, these individuals also reported that family members modeled behavior that allowed them to overcome initial hardship and fostered an interest in service work as a career.

Being an Outcast. Several young professionals ($n = 7$) saw themselves as "outsiders" during childhood. They identified themselves as marginalized because they were immigrants, racial minorities, homosexuals, or poor. Their childhood experiences were characterized by feelings of isolation and emotional separation from the majority culture. With formative years marked by alienation, these individuals became highly sensitive and empathetic toward other marginalized groups. A young professional explained how her experiences as an immigrant heightened her awareness of the difficulties disadvantaged individuals encounter: "As a child growing up, I think that I did experience a lot of insecurity about being new. . . . And I think it made me be really sensitive and respectful of people that I meet, especially the people that I work with because I work with the disadvantaged. I feel like that's really crucial and I'm always conscious of it."

Experiencing the Death of a Parent or Close Friend. Five young professionals also discussed the impact of losing a parent or close friend early in life. Whereas these events could have led to negative outcomes, these individuals framed their losses in such a way that they learned about the ephemeral nature of life. Teaching them that life can be fragile, these events provoked them to consider lifelong perspectives and goals. Practitioners claimed that these experiences caused them to establish priorities, which included a marked desire to make meaningful contributions to others. For example, a medical school student commented on the effect of his father's death at a young age: "Life can be short, which I experienced. And thinking, how do I want this to affect me, or move me. Do I ignore it, or do I let myself feel what it's like? And if I really let myself feel, then a-ha my behavior changes."

Living with a Troubled Family Member. Four young professionals grew up with troubled family members. The mothers of two individuals, for example, suffered severe mental illnesses leaving them physically or emotionally absent. This isolation forced them to take responsibility for themselves, and often for other family members, at an early age. In doing so, they established themselves as caretakers. A nurse explained the impact of her mother's illness: "I really would take on the totality of the problem that was handled or experienced by, certainly first my mother, and then second any other person I might try to help. I had a conception that I should be able to help them. That was overwhelming, but it left me with a pleasure and an attachment to acts of helping."

Two general points should be noted about these practitioners' early hardships. First, their experiences likely required them to be independent at young ages. Either through the physical or emotional absence of parents or because they felt they did not belong to the majority group, they were required to think independently. This type of thinking, particularly because it was grounded in difficult interpersonal experiences, may have stimulated them to contemplate their value systems at unusually young ages. For the individuals we interviewed, these experiences resulted in a sensitivity to others who are disadvantaged and a firm commitment to their welfare. Interestingly, the one young professional who did not experience hardship at a young age claimed that her upbringing strongly emphasized independent thinking and behavior. Perhaps independent thinking with or without childhood suffering motivates commitment to service.

Second, although the practitioners' hardships led to their dedication to others, alternative outcomes could have emerged. These individuals could have distanced themselves from others similar to themselves in an attempt to avoid reliving their experiences. They also could have felt that because of a difficult childhood, they deserved a more indulgent adulthood. Thus it is important to note the striking ways in which these individuals framed their early experiences. They viewed their hardships as opportunities to connect with and assist others going through experiences similar to their own. Indeed, one nurse commented, "Pain helps the character. . . . and stress could make you stronger or it could shatter you. And I think I've experienced some of both. Maybe sometimes shattered parts when they're rebuilt are somehow stronger, or at least wiser."

Having Role Models. Although many young professionals described the hardships they endured early on, they also commented on the values and strong ethical beliefs parents imparted to them at an early age. Through their parents' work and their interactions with others in their home community, they learned about the importance of helping others in need and, as one participant stated, the importance of showing "one human being's responsibility to others." The ways in which they were raised—to treat their neighbors with respect, to drive to the city regularly to pick up trash after work or school, or to send their "extra" Christmas gifts (each child kept only one) to needy children—became ingrained in these practitioners' minds as the "right" way to live and work.

Six young professionals specifically described their parents as role models because of their commitment to service work. These individuals were raised with the understanding that helping the community and pursuing career goals were not separate but could be integrated to make up their life's work. Many practitioners had not realized the impact these family members had on their lives until they started to contemplate how to shape their own careers. For example, a medical school student talked about his grandfather, a doctor who worked with underserved populations. Because most of his patients did not have enough money to pay for treatment, they would often pay in food or gifts. This individual described how this influenced his life as a young child: "I was really aware of how [my grandfather] must have moved people. . . . that's always been another dream of mine, to devote my career to the underserved." A young nurse similarly described the work of her grandmother, a visiting nurse in Manhattan who traveled across the world "reaching out to people from other countries." This individual explained her own service work as a way to "keep this family legacy alive."

Sustained Commitment. As these individuals entered a pivotal stage in their lives—training for and beginning a career—they spoke of several key factors that sustained their continued service work: participation in the Albert Schweitzer Fellowship program, mentors, personal connections with those in need, and religious beliefs. All of the young professionals described how at least one of these factors "widened" their career interests to maintain service as an inherent part of their daily life. The young professionals encountered a range of influential people and support mechanisms that "legitimized" integrating community service work with a more traditional career path. One medical school student mentioned that the fellowship program was a crystallizing experience—an event that brings about an individual's awareness of his calling or purpose in life (Feldman, 1971; Walters and Gardner, 1986). He stated, "[The fellowship program] really solidified for me some of my commitments and beliefs that had been, until then, perhaps more free floating."

The Fellowship Program. Almost all of the young professionals (n = 15) commented on the importance of their training experiences as graduate students and fellows in the Albert Schweitzer Fellowship program. Undoubtedly, as graduate students, they learned crucial skills and techniques in their respective programs. They almost always complained, however, about the isolation from the larger community they felt as classroom students. One individual commented, "I think as a medical student . . . you just sort of sit behind books. And you don't do anything other than learn facts. And I just, I couldn't do that. So I had to do something." The young professionals (n = 12) also lamented the "dry" experience of graduate school, mainly because those around them only seemed to focus on the content, "memorizing facts and taking tests," with minimal attention to the application and practicality of what they were learning. Some of the practitioners asserted that this "tunnel vision" was due to the pressure students felt about their future careers.

In contrast, the Albert Schweitzer Fellowship program is an opportunity for individuals to reconnect with the community and service work. Young professionals described the program as a "complement" to their graduate program, an "outlet" that provided perspective and balance. For example, a nurse commented, "I was looking for something that was going to bring me out of the hospital, out of the classroom, into the community, and health promotion has always been a big interest of mine, so that was one way I could kind of tie my own interest into doing community work."

Specifically, eight practitioners mentioned the importance of being part of a professionally diverse group of individuals that gives them the opportunity to learn about other health-related fields, as well as how these other areas affect and influence those they serve. These new perspectives lead them to consider their patients' emotional, environmental, and physical needs, even if these are not their primary areas of concern. A student training in internal medicine explained this influence of the fellowship program this way: "It also makes me understand how dedicated health care providers need to be. They really have more responsibility than just physical and medical advice. It really comes to the whole psychosocial aspect of patient care, and I think sometimes providers forget about that."

Many individuals (n = 14) shaped, and in some cases reshaped, their future careers in order to maintain the ways in which they worked with patients during the fellowship period. Approaching clients in a more holistic manner or spending extra time communicating with patients to make sure they understand what has been said are two different strategies young professionals mentioned that would or had become part of their daily work.

More generally, almost all of the Schweitzer fellows (n = 14) asserted that because of the validation they received throughout the fellowship, the traditional boundaries of their careers were widened to include service work as a sanctioned element. A few individuals, for example, stated that the application of skills was just one part of their job; there were many other ways they should serve those in need. One young doctor about to start his residency said, "I hesitate to think what would have happened to me if I had gone to medical school and not done the Schweitzer fellowship. Because I think it would have just narrowed it down."

Mentors. Graduate school training also proved helpful to the young professionals (n = 15) for the opportunity to forge meaningful mentor relationships with their advisers, professors, and other physicians. These mentors played a key role in these individuals' enduring commitment to service work in two ways: they supported these practitioners' belief in the value of service work, and they modeled how community work could be integrated with one's career. During a time when these individuals felt isolated from the community and set apart from their peers who were more interested in advancing academically, their mentors provided support and validation for their community interests and future career plans.

A young doctor spoke of a well-known doctor and community worker who served as an important mentor during graduate school through his support of and commitment to similar work. This individual described the significance of having someone in his life with a common understanding: "And, so to have someone that really supports you and says, you know, you can do this, you can keep on going. If you really are true to what you believe in, then keep going because we've done it and we're continually doing what we believe in." For students who often felt dismayed by academicians' and administrators' lack of interest in service work, these mentors were helpful in providing a sense of hope that, as one participant stated, "there are people within academics who are also interested in what happen[s] outside of the ivory tower of academia."

It is important to note that most young professionals seek out particular individuals because they are interested in their work and the ways they carry it out; these mentors are not assigned. Perhaps because the students and mentors share a rare interest in community work, the mentors are genuinely helpful to young practitioners. A social worker described this type of "healthy" relationship: "A good mentor works with you . . . even when they don't get something from you. . . . too many mentors, they work with someone because they get something. They get more out of it than you do."

Relationships with Those in Need. The very individuals the young professionals served were also an important source of strength for them because they knew they had "made a difference" in people's lives. Helping someone move out of a homeless shelter or inspiring an elderly person to have a fresh outlook on life motivated many practitioners (n = 11) to continue with this work. Receiving recognition or acknowledgment from the individuals they served was also inspiring to the young professionals ($n = 10$). A social worker talked about the impact of receiving a card from a patient diagnosed as a paranoid schizophrenic: "[A]ccording to my supervisor, that is the first thing that [the patient] ever completed. Didn't expect it. Didn't ask for it.... the first time I thought I was doing really great social work is when I got this beautiful card from this scared woman."

At least one young nurse, however, talked about the serious "risk" of letting individuals with whom one is working become involved in one's personal life. These individuals mentioned that their desire to reach out to people in need had no boundaries—there were no "days off" in service work. One participant asked, "Where do you draw the line between professional goals and barriers and then personal? I don't know. It's hard." This individual spoke about the "toll" on her personal life exacted by the death of a patient with whom she had become very close over a period of several years. She remarked that "it was [a] really upsetting and draining experience." The only way she made it through the trauma was by relying on religion—her sense of faith in a higher power.

Faith. Nearly all young professionals ($n = 12$) mentioned how faith strengthened their service work. Many of these individuals participated in organized religion, but for some, faith was the calling they felt to help others. Because of the nature of their daily professional work in health and social service—dealing with various ethical issues and questions about life and death—it may seem logical that religious beliefs were important. However, for many of these practitioners, faith was more than a system of beliefs they consulted in difficult situations. Faith was the foundation of their work: it gave them a reason to serve others and supported them in this commitment. One individual stated, "My work is my religion, in a sense. By trying to alleviate suffering, to me that is religion. And I can do that best as a nurse."

For some young professionals, faith was the main reason for doing community service work—even if organized religion was not part of their upbringing. In other words, some individuals sought out specific religious beliefs because they supported dedication to service work and gave them a reason to care for others so deeply. A doctor who became a Christian after the death of his sister explained how his faith in Christ motivated his work: "[B]ecause of my faith in Christ, it's a redeeming, motivating goal to really rectify some of these issues and to take care of children in impoverished states. . . . because I believe that everything else is pale in comparison to doing what I believe I should be doing, and that would be serving the poor." A nurse also explained her more recent involvement in religion: "I'm now more embracing the Catholic Church in large part because of [the] social justice work that they do, that's very powerful to me. I also have embraced the Quaker faith, and a lot of their values, and [I] would like to continue learning more about that."

Even if they were not actively involved in religious institutions, six young professionals maintained that religion and faith played a valuable role, mainly by giving balance and perspective to their lives. Regarding spirituality, a medical school student explained, "[It] rounds me out and makes me feel like I'm giving something back." Others believed that religion and faith provided them with a "point of reference" and a framework not only for serving those in need but for considering ethical issues in their work. Another medical school student explained, "[Religion] influences my ethics in that I think that it's always important to think carefully about all the sort of good and bad outcomes for all the people involved."

Analysis

Through our study of these highly committed, exemplary individuals, we gained insight into factors that are significant in their lives and that are essential to their enduring commitment to service work. These individuals not only identified with caretaking roles from an early age; they also pursued a career path that upheld this service orientation. Some of the experiences they described as instrumental, such as parental role models and meaningful encounters with those in need, resonate with existing literature on community service and social responsibility (Youniss and Yates, 1997; Colby and Damon, 1992). However, for this particular group, experiencing hardships early in their lives was also often described as pivotal in fostering an empathy toward others and an obligation to help those with similar plights. This experience and ability to "reframe" challenges as inspiration was one of the attributes that made this group distinct.

In terms of future work, the practitioners we interviewed seemed hopeful that they would be able to maintain their commitment to service. Many described efforts to expand or deepen their future involvement in service through skill building and networking. Several young professionals attempted to cultivate specific skills that would allow them to better assist those in need, such as learning the native languages and communication styles of those they served. In addition, these individuals often spoke of the importance of networking in the health and social service communities in order to deepen their work and serve a larger community.

At the same time, however, many young professionals also worried about maintaining a balance between service work and interpersonal commitments, such as those to spouses or children. They feared that they could not be sufficiently present for both their own families and for the individuals they served, that a commitment to one would mean failing the other.

At other points in these individuals' lives, however, they persevered through inevitable conflicts that arise for young professionals deeply committed to service work. Many, for example, discussed the difficulty of being a medical school student surrounded by peers, professors, and clinicians solely focused on academic achievement. Practitioners often commented on the helpfulness of the nurturing environments that encouraged and legitimized their desire to serve others during these times. Whether with family members, other Schweitzer fellows, or mentors, individuals developed and sought out supportive networks of people who embodied or endorsed a commitment to the welfare of others.

This finding is most encouraging in considering how to support such individuals who intensely care for others. As parents, supervisors, and academic advisers, we need to value and visibly legitimize service work and help individuals to integrate their professional interests with personal desires to serve others. Schools at all levels, religious institutions, and professional organizations can motivate individuals to become involved by connecting them with other service workers and by offering volunteer opportunities. Just as importantly, they can help sustain individuals' commitment through providing resources, such as space, time, and money. Programs such as the Albert Schweitzer Fellowship program are examples of how independent organizations can also act as catalysts for combining professional interests with a profound sense of responsibility to others. One Schweitzer fellow, who was thankful for the opportunity the program provided, commented, "Wherever I am, there will probably be projects that I'll get involved in. . . . I think this [service work] is a lifelong process that was boosted by the fellowship [program]." Through these kinds of coalitions and alliances, we can provide individuals the support they need—so they can provide the same for those about whom they care so deeply.

Note

1. Names of persons and places pertaining to individuals quoted in this chapter have been changed to ensure confidentiality.

References

Cohen, J. "A Coefficient of Agreement for Nominal Scales." *Educational Psychological Measurement,* 1960, *20,* 37–46.

Colby, A., and Damon, W. *Some Do Care: Contemporary Lives of Moral Commitment.* New York: Free Press, 1992.

Damon, W. *Greater Expectations.* New York: Free Press, 1995.

Feldman, D. H. "Map Understanding as a Possible Crystallizer of Cognitive Structures." *American Educational Research Journal,* 1971, *8,* 485–501.

Gardner, H. *Extraordinary Minds: Portraits of Exceptional Individuals and an Examination of Our Extraordinariness.* New York: Basic Books, 1997.

Kutner, N., and Brogan, D. "The Decision to Enter Medicine: Motivations, Social Support, and Discouragements for Women." *Psychology of Women Quarterly,* 1980, *5,* 341–357.

Powell, A., Boakes, J., and Slater, P. "What Motivates Medical Students: How They See Themselves and Their Profession." *Medical Education,* May 1987, pp. 176–182.

Solomon, D., Watson, M., and Battistich, V. "Teaching and Schools Effects on Moral/Prosocial Development." *Review of Educational Research,* forthcoming.

Walters, J., and Gardner, H. "The Crystallizing Experience: Discovery of an Intellectual Gift." In R. J. Sternberg and J. E. Davidson (eds.), *Conceptions of Giftedness.* New York: Cambridge University Press, 1986.

Youniss, J., and Yates, M. *Community Service and Social Responsibility in Youth.* Chicago: University of Chicago Press, 1997.

WENDY FISCHMAN manages the origins study of the Good Work Project, Harvard Graduate School of Education.

DEBORAH A. SCHUTTE is a doctoral candidate at Harvard Graduate School of Education and a researcher for the origins study of the Good Work Project, Harvard Graduate School of Education.

BECCA SOLOMON manages the Dedicated Young Professionals study of the Good Work Project, Harvard Graduate School of Education.

GRACE WU LAM is a former researcher for the origins study of the Good Work Project, Harvard Graduate School of Education.

4

This chapter explores factors that predict adolescent participation in cooperative activities, which may indicate a predisposition to become involved in community activities later in life. It specifically examines the idea that middle schoolers' subjective experience of challenge may be linked to cooperative behavior later in adolescence.

Predictors of Positive Cooperative Behavior in Youths

Hugh McIntosh, Jennifer A. Schmidt, Fengbin Chang

Conventional wisdom and empirical research suggest that youth engagement in cooperative activities like clubs, youth groups, and sports is beneficial not only to a child's development but also to society. Many educators and parents view such after-school activities as beneficial because they "keep kids off the street and out of trouble." They reason that children on the ball field or at the community center have fewer opportunities to engage in less productive, potentially harmful activities. These assumptions are largely supported by empirical research. Although the process by which cooperative engagement influences well-being may be more complex than "keeping kids off the street," several studies have established links between participation in clubs, hobbies, sports, and community service and desirable personal outcomes, such as reduced delinquency, reduced absenteeism, higher academic grades, higher levels of self-esteem, and increased initiative (Eccles and Barber, 1999; Larson, 1994, 2000; Marsh, 1992; Rachman, 1979; Raymore, Barber, Eccles, and Godbey, 1999; Schmidt, 1998; Werner, 1993; Werner and Smith, 1992).

Empirical evidence supports common assumptions about the long-term societal benefits of youth participation as well. An accumulating body of

The authors wish to thank Barbara Schneider and Mihaly Csikszentmihalyi for their helpful comments on earlier drafts of this chapter. Preparation of this chapter was supported by the Alfred P. Sloan Center on Parents, Children, and Work and the National Science Foundation (Grant #REC-9725509). This study is intended to promote the exchange of ideas among researchers, practitioners, and policymakers. The views expressed here are those of the authors and do not represent those of their institutions or granting institutions.

research links participation in organized youth activities during high school with involvement in community, religious, and political organizations during adulthood (Beane, Turner, Jones, and Lipka, 1981; Hanks and Eckland, 1978; Ladewig and Thomas, 1987; Otto, 1976; Verba, Schlozman, and Brady, 1995; for a review see Youniss, McLellan, and Yates, 1997). These studies suggest that participation in cooperative activities during adolescence may establish behavior patterns and a commitment to shared goals that continue through adulthood. Recognizing this connection, researchers have proposed various structured youth activities to encourage cooperative behavior in an attempt to ensure a more civically and socially engaged society in the future (Putnam, 2000; Stukas, Clary, and Snyder, 1999).

Given the potential personal and societal benefits of youth participation in cooperative activities, we would like to know which adolescents become engaged in cooperative activities and what motivates them to do so. For example, do teenagers from certain demographic, socioeconomic, or religious backgrounds tend to participate at higher levels in such activities? Beyond knowing more about background characteristics, which may largely reflect differences in access to such opportunities, we would like to understand how adolescents' early subjective experiences may shape their cooperative behavior later in adolescence. Such knowledge would help parents, educators, and community leaders identify experiential influences that encourage teenagers to participate in activities that may promote positive behavioral and psychological outcomes in the present and that could lead to more civic or social engagement in the future.

Motivation for Cooperative Behavior

Although research has found links between cooperative behaviors and positive outcomes, we know little about what factors, experiences, and processes motivate adolescents to engage in these activities. When children are young, parents can encourage or even force them to participate in youth groups, sports teams, and community service projects. But by the time they reach late adolescence, teens likely participate in such activities largely by choice. What types of individuals, then, find themselves drawn to these kinds of activities?

Research on intrinsic motivation has identified challenge as a distinct mode of experience through which individuals sustain interest in activities. Persons are more likely to persist in activities that continually present new opportunities to stretch their abilities just a little further (Csikszentmihalyi, 1990; Csikszentmihalyi, Rathunde, and Whalen, 1993; Jackson and Csikszentmihalyi, 1999; Massimini and Delle Fave, 2000; Whalen, 1993). Sports, clubs, and other cooperative activities provide clear goals and challenges within the structure of the activity at hand (Jackson and Csikszentmihalyi, 1999). In sports the challenge is often to defeat an opponent while operating within the rules of the game. Interest and hobby clubs present such challenges as finding the right exposure for a photograph or building a radio that actually works. In youth groups and community service, challenges may be less obvious but usually involve working together toward a mutual goal, such as a service project or a shared learning experience. A common feature of all these activities is a shared goal, where the challenges for meeting that goal are usually well defined.

Learning how to create or find challenge in the absence of externally imposed structure is important for continued development and interest in any area of involvement (Whalen, 1993). Take, for example, the composer who sets personal goals about how to use instruments, words, and music to elicit increasingly complex emotions. If she does not set such goals and continually writes simple songs that do not challenge her ability, she is likely to lose interest in her work because it will soon become repetitive and boring. Individuals can identify, and even create, challenges outside the structure of cooperative activities. But in activities like team sports, clubs, and service projects, the challenges and goals are inherent to the activity.

Much of the research on challenge already mentioned is based on the idea that there is an "optimal" level of challenge that is most conducive to learning, growth, or sustained interest (for reviews see Csikszentmihalyi, 1990; Whalen, 1993). When challenges are too low, there is no opportunity for action or development; the activity becomes boring, and the individual may lose interest in it. Conversely, if an activity is too challenging, the individual may feel overwhelmed and lose interest because the task is too difficult. Optimal challenge (neither too high nor too low) has been linked to positive workplace experiences (LeFevre, 1988), task persistence (Bandura, 1990), academic development (Nakamura, 1988), talent development (Csikszentmihalyi, Rathunde, and Whalen, 1993), and resilience (Maddi and Kobasa, 1981, 1984; Schmidt, 1998). This idea—that a moderate level of challenge is optimal for development, growth, and sustained interest—informs several influential theories of human development, including theories of optimal discrepancy and achievement approach motives (McClelland, Atkinson, Clark, and Lowell, 1953), dialectical equilibration (Piaget, 1967), and proximal zone of development (Vygotsky, 1978).

Research Questions

Our study first provides a descriptive analysis of adolescents' subjective experience of challenge in daily life: Which activities, on average, are perceived as most challenging? Next we attempt to answer the following question: Are middle schoolers who experience moderate levels of challenge (neither too high nor too low) more likely as high schoolers to participate in cooperative activities, such as youth groups, sports, and service? We then explore the relationship between demographic variables, such as gender and religiosity, on the one hand and participation in positive cooperative activities on the other.

Method

Data used for our analyses were collected in 1992–1993 (year 1) and 1996–1997 (year 5) by the Alfred P. Sloan Study of Youth and Social Development, a national longitudinal study of career development. The Sloan study gathered data from sixth, eighth, tenth, and twelfth graders at middle schools and high schools in a dozen U.S. localities selected to represent urban, suburban, and rural areas and to achieve a racially, ethnically, and socioeconomically diverse sample (for a full description of the study, see Csikszentmihalyi and Schneider, 2000). During years 1 and 5, participants were studied using the Experience Sampling Method (ESM); they also completed the Teenage Life Questionnaire (TLQ) and other surveys.

Experience Sampling Method. The ESM is designed to document participants' behavior, moods, and thoughts over a week. Programmed wristwatches randomly signal subjects eight times daily between 7:30 A.M. and 10:30 P.M. (Csikszentmihalyi and Larson, 1984; Csikszentmihalyi and Schneider, 2000). The schedule of signals is unpredictable to respondents while providing a representative sample of moods and activities for the week. In response to each signal, participants are to record their activities and feelings on a short self-report form and rate the challenge of their current activity on a 9-point scale.

Teenage Life Questionnaire. The TLQ includes modified questions from the National Education Longitudinal Study of 1988–94 (for the study design see Hafner, Ingels, Schneider, and Stevenson, 1990). The TLQ provides demographic information about students, documents their school experiences, and asks questions about the amount of time they spend in various extracurricular activities. We were particularly interested in a subset of questions focused on participation in nonschool cooperative leisure activities: attending youth groups or recreational programs, volunteering or performing community service, and playing nonschool sports (either formally organized outside of school or informal pickup games) with friends. We selected these three dependent variables assuming that adolescents would make a more personal choice about becoming involved in such activities than they might about participating in other nonschool activities such as paid work, homework, and extracurricular school activities, where economic, academic, social, and other pressures might be more influential.

A word about calling sports a cooperative activity may be warranted. Sports differ from the other activities examined here because they are simultaneously cooperative and competitive. Playing ball or other team sports involves relatively high levels of cooperation, particularly with informal pickup games. The cooperation that adolescents display in executing a double play in softball, for example, is often superb. Even in nonteam sports, such as one-on-one basketball, participants must cooperate to establish and enforce the rules of the game. Recall, however, that the sports examined here are limited to those that involve friends, thus ensuring that the experience will require some sort of cooperative interaction.

Sample

Our study uses ESM and TLQ data on students who were in grade 6 or 8 (ages eleven to fourteen) during year 1 and who were surveyed again four years later, when they were in grade 10 or 12 (ages fifteen to eighteen). In year 1, 1,214 students were surveyed, including 317 sixth graders and 347 eighth graders. Of these 664 middle schoolers, 227 were surveyed again as high schoolers in year 5. From this initial sample of 227, we excluded students who in year 1 responded fewer than ten times to the ESM challenge item or had no variation on this measure. The final sample included 204 students.

The Concept of Challenge

As stated earlier, ratings of challenge in this study are subjective. We focus on subjective challenge rather than on specific activities in order to capture instances when adolescents find challenges in circumstances that may not on the surface seem challenging. Take, for example, the youth who listens to music and tries to follow the percussion line throughout the piece. Although "listening to music" may not appear to be a very challenging activity, the way our hypothetical teen has chosen to listen (focusing only on the percussion while mentally tuning out the other instrument lines) could present substantial challenges.

Even though our analyses focus on adolescents' subjective experience of challenge, we want to know whether adolescents' perceptions of challenge are generally tied to particular activities. Figure 4.1 presents students' mean challenge ratings in year 1 while doing various activities, such as watching television, talking with friends, or doing schoolwork. Not surprisingly, Figure 4.1 indicates that subjective ratings of challenge largely depend on the type of activity. On average, adolescents perceive academic schoolwork and extracurricular activities as highly challenging, whereas passive activities like watching television and personal maintenance (brushing hair, eating) are typically experienced as least challenging. Nonacademic schoolwork (art, music, and other elective courses) falls into the middle range of the challenge distribution. Remember that Figure 4.1 presents averages and that the challenge level of any activity may be perceived differently by different adolescents. Nevertheless, as we discuss our results, it may be helpful to keep these concrete activities in mind as exemplars of low-, moderate-, and high-challenge activities.

Because we wanted to understand the relationship between challenge and voluntary participation in cooperative activity, we decided to focus on subjective challenge ratings in activities in which students chose to participate. Although school is one of the most challenging daily activities for teenagers, it is compulsory. Therefore challenge measures used in the following analyses exclude all responses that occurred when participants were

Figure 4.1. Adolescents' Mean Subjective Challenge Ratings for Selected Activities in Year 1

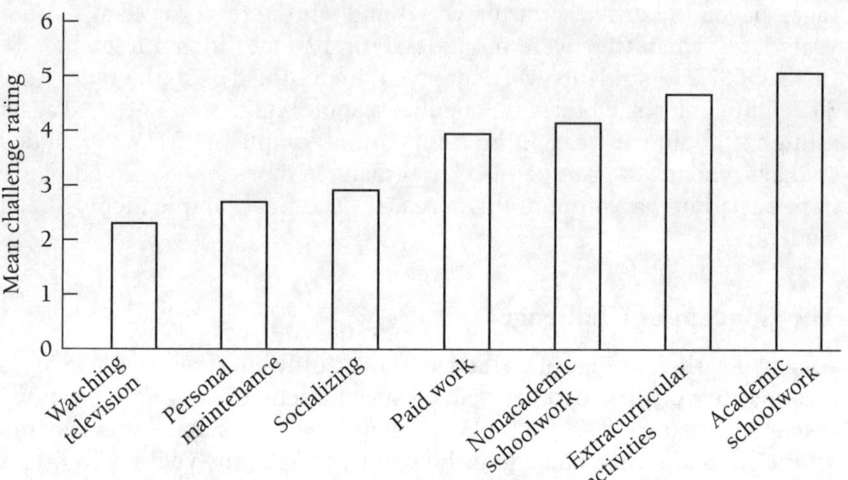

Note: For each activity a 95 percent confidence interval is indicated by the line extending above and below the activity's mean.

in school. For each person, then, we computed the average challenge score for all nonschool responses.

This average score essentially captures two dimensions of challenge. One is the willingness of adolescents to engage in challenge. We can assume that teenagers exercise some choice over which nonschool activities they participate in and that they choose activities with a level of challenge acceptable to them. In addition, the challenge score captures the total level of challenge in youths' nonschool experiences. For our analyses we trichotomized challenge scores into high, moderate, and low groups.

Results

Table 4.1 presents the mean rates of student participation in various nonschool activities in year 5 relative to a set of year-1 student characteristics. The table presents mean participation in youth groups, service activities, and nonschool sports independently; it also examines cooperative participation generally by summing the participation levels of all three types of activities.

The data indicate only a few significant differences in participation levels by the demographic factors examined here. Males participated in sports at higher rates than females. Students who were more religious and those whose parents were more highly educated participated in youth groups at higher rates than other adolescents. More-religious students also were more

Table 4.1. Mean Student Participation in Nonschool Leisure Activities in Year 5

Variable in Year 1	*n*	*Group*	*Service*	*Sports*	*Cooperative*
Gender					
Male	75	0.52	0.19	0.83[†]	1.51
Female	129	0.57	0.35	0.40[‡]	1.30
Race/ethnicity					
White	138	0.58	0.33	0.61	1.49
Nonwhite[a]	66	0.49	0.22	0.40	1.07
Parent education					
No four-year degree	65	0.27[†]	0.23	0.58	1.05
Four-year degree	68	0.61[‡]	0.34	0.66	1.58
Advanced degree	69	0.73[‡]	0.32	0.41	1.45
Grades					
C's and D's or worse	6	0.75	0.88	0.50	2.13
B's and C's or mostly C's	38	0.48	0.25	0.64	1.34
A's and B's or mostly B's	69	0.51	0.21	0.59	1.27
Mostly A's	83	0.62	0.36	0.52	1.49
Religiosity					
Not religious	57	0.31[†]	0.22	0.38	0.89[†]
Somewhat religious	113	0.57[†]	0.30	0.62	1.43[†]
Very religious	24	0.97[‡]	0.38	0.60	2.00[‡]
Challenge outside of school					
Low	86	0.47[†]	0.33	0.44	1.19[†]
Moderate	49	0.95[‡]	0.34	0.68	1.97[‡]
High	56	0.40[†]	0.22	0.63	1.24[†]

Note: For group, service, and sports activities, 0 = rarely or never, 0.5 = less than once a week, and 1.5 = once a week or more. Cooperative activities combines group, service, and sports activity values in a scale ranging from 0 to 4.5. Means with the same superscript (either a dagger or a double dagger) are not significantly different; means with different superscripts are significantly different, $p < .05$.

[a] Asian American, Hispanic American, and African American.

likely than other students to participate in cooperative activities in general (group, service, and sports activities combined). No significant differences in participation in service activities emerged for any of the independent variables. This may be due to the fact that, in general, teens tended to participate in service activities far less often than in youth groups or sports.

Results for the challenge variables suggest a link between challenge in year 1 and participation in cooperative activities in year 5. For cooperative activities in general and youth groups in particular, students who experienced moderate challenge in year 1 participated at substantially higher rates than high-challenge or low-challenge students. This pattern holds for participation in service and sports, though the differences between challenge groups are not statistically significant.

Table 4.2. Odds of Student Participation in Nonschool Cooperative Activities in Year 5

Independent Variable in Year 1	*Group*	*Service*	*Sports*
Year-1 participation (yes versus no)	4.80**	2.85*	12.05***
Gender (versus male)			
Female	1.10	1.13	0.26**
Race/ethnicity (versus white)			
Nonwhite	1.71	0.85	0.38
Parent education (versus no four-year degree)			
Four-year degree	1.79	1.63	0.91
Advanced degree	3.20*	1.21	0.38
Grades	1.33	1.60	1.73
Religiosity (versus not religious)			
Somewhat religious	4.25**	1.76	2.02
Very religious	24.08**	1.43	0.66
Challenge outside of school (versus low)			
Moderate	4.55**	1.08	5.13**
High	0.56	0.66	3.28*

Note: Log odds (the typical output of logistic regression) were transformed to relative odds by taking the exponential of each regression coefficient.

[a] In years 1 and 5, participation in groups, service, and sports is coded yes versus no. Yes = less than once a week, or once a week or more. No = rarely or never.

*$p < .05$. **$p < .01$. ***$p < .001$ (two-tailed tests).

To better understand the multiple factors that predict involvement in youth groups, community service, and sports, we used logistic regression analysis to estimate the likelihood of participating in each of these activities. Logistic regression allows us to estimate the relative contribution of each independent variable in the model, keeping other variables in the model constant. The coefficients reported in Table 4.2 indicate the relative odds of participation (versus nonparticipation) in each activity in year 5, controlling on year-1 participation.

Group Activities. Table 4.2 shows that previous youth group participation, parent education, and religiosity predicted participation in youth groups. Students whose parents had advanced degrees were over three times more likely ($p < .05$) to participate in youth groups than their peers with less-educated parents. The odds of youth group participation were over four times greater ($p < .01$) for somewhat religious adolescents and over twenty-four times greater ($p < .01$) for very religious adolescents compared with their nonreligious peers.

As expected, the experience of moderate challenge in middle school also predicted student involvement in youth groups and recreational programs during high school. Controlling on all other factors, students who as sixth or eighth graders experienced moderate challenge in their daily lives were four and a half times more likely to participate in group activities in high school than students who experienced low levels of challenge ($p < .01$).

Service Activities. Previous participation in service proved to be the only significant predictor of year-5 service participation. Students who were involved in community service in year 1 were nearly three times more likely than their peers to be involved in service again in year 5 ($p < .05$).

Sports Activities. Previous sports participation, gender, and challenge all predicted year-5 participation in nonschool sports. Females were about one-fourth as likely as males to participate in sports in their free time ($p < .01$).

The relationship between year-1 challenge and sports participation was as expected. Compared with low-challenge students, the odds of sports participation were over five times greater for moderate-challenge students ($p < .01$). High-challenge students were also more likely than low-challenge students to engage in sports ($p < .05$), but the highest participation rates were observed among moderate-challenge individuals.

Cooperative Activities in General. As our primary goal was to identify precursors to cooperative engagement across a range of activities, we undertook analyses to predict year-5 participation levels in cooperative activities generally (groups + sports + service). We used ordinary least squares regression analyses to predict cooperative activity participation using independent variables identical to those in Table 4.2, including a year-1 participation variable to control for previous involvement in cooperative activities. The results are shown in Table 4.3. Because the outcome measure is now continuous, the regression coefficients in Table 4.3 represent absolute increases or decreases in participation rates rather than odds of participation.

As expected, prior participation in cooperative activities predicted participation in year 5. Our results show strong effects for religiosity and challenge on participation in cooperative activities generally. Students who identified themselves as somewhat or very religious had higher participation rates in cooperative activities compared with their nonreligious peers.

Controlling on other factors, the relationship between challenge and participation in cooperative activities is clearly curvilinear. Young teens who experienced moderate levels of challenge became more involved in cooperative activities later in adolescence compared with their peers who perceived low or high challenge. Including challenge as a predictor boosts the explanatory power of the regression model by over 20 percent, as measured by an increase in the R^2 from .24 to .29 (the first model is not shown).

Table 4.3. Ordinary Least Squares Regression Model for Student Participation in Nonschool Cooperative Activities in Year 5

Independent Variable in Year 1	*Coefficient*
Year-1 participation	0.32**
Gender (versus male)	
Female	–0.21
Race/ethnicity (versus white)	
Nonwhite	–0.22
Parent education (versus no four-year degree)	
Four-year degree	0.23
Advanced degree	–0.03
Grades	0.19
Religiosity (versus not religious)	
Somewhat religious	0.52*
Very religious	0.92**
Challenge outside of school (versus low)	
Moderate	0.65*
High	0.05
R^2	0.29

Note: This variable combines values for group, service, and sports activities in a scale ranging from 0 to 4.5. For group, service, and sports activities, 0 = rarely or never, 0.5 = less than once a week, and 1.5 = once a week or more.

$*p < .05$. $**p < .01$. $***p < .001$ (two-tailed tests).

Discussion

We begin discussion of our findings with some cautionary words about interpretation. First, these data are drawn from a study that examined a limited set of cooperative activities, and our findings may have limited application to activities beyond those studied here. Second, the sample size is relatively small, and consequently the statistical power of our tests is limited. We therefore will occasionally refer to patterns in data that have not reached statistical significance yet suggest a particular result. Third, the small sample size may have particularly affected our ability to identify predictors of participation in community service, which is much less common than participation in youth groups or sports (see Table 4.1). Thus our findings cannot be considered conclusive without replication in larger adolescent populations, with more-comprehensive measures of cooperative activity.

Nonetheless, the unique methodology employed in this study, along with the longitudinal design, has allowed us to explore the way adolescents perceive challenge in their daily lives and to examine the effects of those experiences on later cooperative behavior. Our findings about the relationship between early exposure to challenge and later engagement in cooperative activities are robust and consistent with our hypothesis.

Demographic Correlates of Cooperative Behavior. The relationships between background characteristics and participation in cooperative activities are not surprising and, for the most part, reflect commonly recognized gender differences and religious practices. Girls participate in nonschool sports far less frequently than boys do. Although federal legislation was enacted nearly three decades ago requiring schools to give females and males equal chances in athletics, girls may still have fewer opportunities to play sports in nonschool settings. Girls may also spread their involvement among a wider range of activities (as indicated by slightly higher participation in service and group activities), whereas boys tend to cluster in sports. Table 4.3, however, indicates that gender is not a significant predictor of cooperative participation generally. This finding suggests that although they may choose different types of cooperative activities, boys and girls engage in cooperative activities overall at roughly equal rates.

Similar conclusions may be drawn about the effects of race/ethnicity and parent education on participation in cooperative activities. Table 4.2 suggests that nonwhite adolescents are only about one-third as likely as their white peers to participate in nonschool sports. (In this and the following example, interpretations are based in part on participation differences that, though falling short of statistical significance here, may become more robust in larger samples.) Table 4.2 also indicates that parent education is related to increased participation in youth groups and may be related to decreased participation in sports. For cooperative activities overall, however, such differences are much smaller (see Table 4.3). Together, these results indicate that adolescents from different racial, ethnic, or socioeconomic backgrounds may tend to participate in different types of cooperative activities but that their rates of participation in cooperative activities overall are about equal. These subtle relationships between race/ethnicity, parent education, and specific cooperative behaviors should be addressed in future research.

Religiosity strongly predicts year-5 engagement in cooperative activities overall. The bulk of this effect is driven by the relationship between religiosity and participation in youth groups, many of which are probably religiously based. This connection between religiosity and cooperative activity in adolescence is not surprising in light of research on cooperative participation involving adults. Religion has been linked to increased civic activity throughout American history (Putnam, 2000). And religious organizations today are a major source of recruits for community-organizing efforts aimed at revitalizing impoverished neighborhoods (Chaskin, Brown, Venkatesh, and Vidal, 2001).

Experiential Correlates of Cooperative Behavior. Together, our regression models show consistent effects for challenge in year 1 on year-5 participation in cooperative activities. These effects persist even after controlling on gender, race, and other background characteristics. The analyses presented in Tables 4.2 and 4.3 reveal that middle schoolers who on average experienced moderate levels of daily challenge participated more often in an array of cooperative behaviors as high schoolers. Because these longitudinal analyses control for year-1 participation, the results indicate that moderate-challenge students increased their participation over time relative to their peers.

Overall, these analyses suggest that youths who show a willingness to engage in challenge tend to get involved in cooperative activities. Those whose lives are highly challenging, however, may have less "space" in their lives for the additional challenges offered by extracurricular activities; they may therefore participate in cooperative activities at lower rates than youths whose lives present a moderate level of challenge. Our analyses support the "optimal challenge" hypothesis, which states that children who experience moderate (as opposed to high or low) levels of challenge in their daily lives are more likely to engage in positive cooperative activities later in adolescence.

The relationship between challenge and participation in sports differs slightly from our general findings in that both high and moderate challenge are significantly related to increased participation (see Table 4.2). One possible explanation for this unexpected finding is that enjoyment in sports is generally so high that it draws teens with a variety of previous experiences. In other words, high-challenge youths may be discouraged from participating in some types of cooperate activities but choose to participate in sports because they are so enjoyable. Indeed, post hoc comparisons of ESM reports of enjoyment in a variety of activities reveal that sports are one of the most enjoyable activities for most teens (these results are not shown here).

Another possible explanation is that sports may differ from other activities examined here in that they are both competitive and cooperative. It is conceivable that the relationship between challenge and participation might work somewhat differently for activities that have a competitive element. Some individuals may have a unique preference for high challenges, and these individuals may be particularly drawn to competitive activities because of the potential for high challenge that competition often provides. The effect of early challenge on competitive involvement later in life is another area for future study.

Possible Pathways to Cooperative Engagement. Although our study focused on experienced challenge, other pathways to engagement in cooperative youth activities likely exist. Our analyses revealed, for example, that religiosity is an important predictor of cooperative behavior, and this finding may reflect the existence of a distinct pathway into cooperative activities. Some youths may join cooperative activities because of the challenges they provide, whereas others may participate either because such activities are more readily available through their religious organization or because participation is common among people who share their faith. Thus activity participation may result from individual interests and talents (as suggested by our challenge findings) or may reflect adherence to a particular meaning system (as suggested by our religiosity findings). Other pathways to cooperative participation may exist as well. In a study of parental influences on youth participation in extracurricular activities, Fletcher, Elder, and Mekos (2000) identified two pathways similar to those proposed here, one based on children's interests and another based on parental modeling of community involvement. The existence of these multiple pathways to cooperative engagement is still highly speculative, and further research is necessary to clarify and understand these distinct pathways.

Conclusion

Although it is too early to know whether the adolescents in this study who participated at high rates in cooperative activities will someday become engaged in their communities at similarly high rates, other research cited here suggests they might. The present study can make no guarantees about future civic or social commitment, but our analyses do suggest that one way to encourage and sustain cooperative behavior during adolescence is to provide opportunities for younger children to challenge their abilities. Taken as a whole, these analyses suggest that the experience of moderate challenge is optimal for encouraging cooperative engagement among adolescents.

The subjective experience of challenge, regardless of activity, appears to be an important factor in sustaining commitment to cooperative activities. The fact that individuals may perceive the same activity differently in terms of challenge will be frustrating to some who are looking for easy solutions to get adolescents involved. The bad news is that there is not one prescription for all teens—what could be challenging for one may not be challenging for another. This is also good news. The fact that activities present different challenges to different individuals essentially ensures that adolescents will develop sustained interest in different types of activities and will grow up to fill different roles in society. It is up to parents and educators to help children and adolescents identify activities and develop the ability to challenge themselves in ways that will keep them coming back to positive cooperative behavior.

References

Bandura, A. "Reflections on Non-Ability Determinants of Competence." In R. J. Sternberg and J. Kolligian (eds.), *Competence Considered.* New Haven, Conn.: Yale University Press, 1990.

Beane, J., Turner, J., Jones, D., and Lipka, R. "Long-Term Effects of Community Service Programs." *Curriculum Inquiry,* 1981, *11*(2), 143–155.

Chaskin, R., Brown, P., Venkatesh, S., and Vidal, A. *Building Community Capacity.* Hawthorne, N.Y.: Aldine de Gruyter, 2001.

Csikszentmihalyi, M. *Flow: The Psychology of Optimal Experience.* New York: HarperCollins, 1990.

Csikszentmihalyi, M., and Larson, R. *Being Adolescent: Conflict and Growth in the Teenage Years.* New York: Basic Books, 1984.

Csikszentmihalyi, M., Rathunde, K., and Whalen, S. *Talented Teenagers: The Roots of Success and Failure.* New York: Cambridge University Press, 1993.

Csikszentmihalyi, M., and Schneider, B. *Becoming Adult: How Teenagers Prepare for the World of Work.* New York: Basic Books, 2000.

Eccles, J. S., and Barber, B. L. "Student Council, Volunteering, Basketball, or Marching Band: What Kind of Extracurricular Involvement Really Matters?" *Journal of Adolescent Research,* 1999, *14*(1) 10–43.

Fletcher, A., Elder, G. H., Jr., and Mekos, D. "Parental Influences on Adolescent Involvement in Community Activities." *Journal of Research on Adolescence,* 2000, *10*(1), 29–48.

Hafner, A., Ingels, S., Schneider, B., and Stevenson, D. *A Profile of the American Eighth Grader.* Washington, D.C.: U.S. Department of Education, 1990.

Hanks, M., and Eckland, B. K. "Adult Voluntary Associations and Adolescent Socialization." *Sociology Quarterly,* 1978, *19*(3), 481–490.

Jackson, S. A., and Csikszentmihalyi, M. *Flow in Sports: The Keys to Optimal Experiences and Performances.* Champaign, Ill.: Human Kinetics, 1999.

Ladewig, H., and Thomas, J. K. *Assessing the Impact of 4-H on Former Members.* College Station: Texas A&M University, 1987.

Larson, R. "Youth Organizations, Hobbies, and Sports as Developmental Contexts." In R. K. Silbereisen and E. Todt (eds.), *Adolescence in Context: The Interplay of Family, School, Peers, and Work in Adjustment.* New York: Springer-Verlag, 1994.

Larson, R. "Toward a Psychology of Positive Youth Development." *American Psychologist,* 2000, *55*(1), 170–183.

LeFevre, J. "Flow and the Quality of Experience During Work and Leisure." In M. Csikszentmihalyi and I. S. Csikszentmihalyi (eds.), *Optimal Experience: Psychological Studies of Flow in Consciousness.* New York: Cambridge University Press, 1988.

Maddi, S. R., and Kobasa, S. C. "Intrinsic Motivation and Health." In H. I. Day (ed.), *Advances in Intrinsic Motivation and Aesthetics.* New York: Plenum Press, 1981.

Maddi, S. R., and Kobasa, S. C. *The Hardy Executive: Health Under Stress.* Homewood, Ill.: Dorsey Press, 1984.

Marsh, H. W. "Extracurricular Activities: Beneficial Extension of the Traditional Curriculum or Subversion of Academic Goals?" *Journal of Educational Psychology,* 1992, *84*(4), 553–562.

Massimini, F., and Delle Fave, A. "Individual Development in a Bio-Cultural Perspective." *American Psychologist,* 2000, *55*(1), 24–33.

McClelland, D. C., Atkinson, J. W., Clark, R. A., and Lowell, E. L. *The Achievement Motive.* Englewood Cliffs, N.J.: Appleton-Century-Crofts, 1953.

Nakamura, J. "Optimal Experience and the Uses of Talent." In M. Csikszentmihalyi and I. S. Csikszentmihalyi (eds.), *Optimal Experience: Psychological Studies of Flow in Consciousness.* New York: Cambridge University Press, 1988.

Otto, L. B. "Social Integration and the Status-Attainment Process." *American Journal of Sociology,* 1976, *81*(6), 1360–1383.

Piaget, J. *Six Psychological Studies.* New York: Vintage Books, 1967.

Putnam, R. D. *Bowling Alone: The Collapse and Revival of American Community.* New York: Simon & Schuster, 2000.

Rachman, S. "The Concept of Required Helpfulness." *Behavior and Research Therapy,* 1979, *17*(1), 1–6.

Raymore, L. A., Barber, B. L., Eccles, J. S., and Godbey, G. C. "Leisure Behavior Pattern Stability During the Transition from Adolescence to Young Adulthood." *Journal of Youth and Adolescence,* 1999, *28*(1), 79–103.

Schmidt, J. "Overcoming Challenges: Exploring the Role of Action, Experience, and Opportunity in Fostering Resilience Among Adolescents." Unpublished doctoral dissertation, University of Chicago, 1998.

Stukas, A. A., Jr., Clary, G., and Snyder, M. "Service Learning: Who Benefits and Why." *Social Policy Report,* 1999, *113*(4), 1–19.

Verba, S., Schlozman, K. L., and Brady, H. E. *Voice and Equality: Civic Voluntarism in American Politics.* Cambridge, Mass.: Harvard University Press, 1995.

Vygotsky, L. *Mind in Society.* Cambridge, Mass.: Harvard University Press, 1978.

Werner, E. E. "Risk, Resilience, and Recovery: Perspectives from the Kauai Longitudinal Study." *Development and Psychopathology,* 1993, *5*(1), 503–515.

Werner, E. E., and Smith, R. S. *Overcoming the Odds: High Risk Children from Birth to Adulthood.* Ithaca, N.Y.: Cornell University Press, 1992.

Whalen, S. "Preference for Challenge and the Development of Talent During Adolescence." Unpublished doctoral dissertation, University of Chicago, 1993.

Youniss, J., McLellan, J. A., and Yates, M. "What We Know About Engendering Civic Identity." *American Behavioral Scientist,* 1997, *40*(5), 620–631.

HUGH MCINTOSH recently completed a master's degree in the social sciences at the University of Chicago.

JENNIFER A. SCHMIDT is research director for the Alfred P. Sloan Center on Parents, Children, and Work at the University of Chicago.

FENGBIN CHANG is a doctoral candidate in sociology at the University of Chicago and a research associate at the National Opinion Research Center.

5

Mentors of novice scientists play an important role in fostering protégés' sense of commitment to science. As this sense of commitment deepens, protégés may come to value serving as mentors themselves, a phenomenon dubbed "mentorship reciprocity."

Encouraging Mentorship in Young Scientists

Gregory C. Feldman

Mentoring relationships, common in nearly all professions, are central in the training of scientists. Studies of elite scientific lineages reveal that mentors teach protégés how to select important problems for investigation and design experiments that will have an impact on the field (Kanigel, 1986; Zuckerman, 1977). Young scientists' productivity is positively affected by working with mentors who publish frequently (McGinnis, 1980). Mentors have been shown to contribute to the retention of underrepresented populations in the sciences (Bird, 1994). Mentors are also viewed as teachers and role models of ethical scientific conduct (Alberts and Shine, 1994; Bird, 1994; Djerassi, 1991; Roberts and Sprague, 1995). Findings from this study of novice geneticists suggest two additional benefits of mentoring in science: the deepening of protégés' commitment to the scientific pursuit and the cultivation of an appreciation for mentoring others, referred to here as "mentorship reciprocity."

A seventh-year genetics graduate student in a prestigious M.D.-Ph.D. program attested to these two roles of mentors. He was grateful to his three mentors. He commented that they had each had a profound influence on his development as a scientist and specifically on one of his own career goals: "I need to teach. Because there's not much I can do for [my mentors].

I wish to acknowledge the Christian A. Johnson Endeavor Foundation for its generous financial support of this study; Marcy LeLacheur, Sara Simeone, and Becca Solomon for their roles in the collection and analysis of these data; and Howard Gardner for his helpful comments on an earlier draft of this chapter. This research was conducted as part of the Good Work Project at the Harvard University Graduate School of Education.

Because they're pretty much where they are going to get. So I have to do for other people what they did for me." He was thankful his mentors had convinced him to pursue a scientific career. He added, "I've been very fortunate not to have a bad mentor," explaining that a discouraging mentor could easily have derailed his commitment to the discipline.

This study is an examination of a group of exceptional novice scientists who are either in the final phases of training or in an early professional position in genetics. The focus is on their experiences with mentors—defined as the individuals who guide, nurture, or inspire a young person to achieve a level of personal integrity or professional skill. The impact of "antimentors," individuals who impede the achievement or development of a novice professional, was also investigated. To understand the impact of mentoring and antimentoring relationships on scientists' commitment to their professional pursuit, I will contrast their experiences of mentorship with a similar group of young journalists. I will then return to the sample of novice geneticists to demonstrate that mentoring relationships in early phases of career development can foster greater mentorship reciprocity. I begin by briefly reviewing the relevant literature.

Literature on Mentoring Relationships

Literature on mentoring addresses three important areas that are relevant to this study: the importance of mentoring in attracting and retaining new talent in professional domains, the influence of mentors on protégés' desire to eventually assume the role of mentor, and the developmental stages through which a mentoring relationship evolves.

Mentorship as Attracting and Supporting Talent in Professional Domains. Young professionals benefit from finding in their chosen fields mentors who convey faith in their abilities and support their contributions (Csikszentmihalyi, 1996). Mentorship is also crucial for the maintenance of thriving domains (for example, genetics). A novice's successful entry into a field can benefit from receiving the support of the field in the form of mentorship; the field—and ultimately the domain of knowledge itself—will not thrive if it fails to attract and retain talented new practitioners (Gardner, Csikszentmihalyi, and Damon, 2001). The quality of mentorship in a given domain influences the quality of its future advancements.

Mentorship Reciprocity. The notion of mentorship reciprocity has been supported in past surveys linking early experience as a protégé with later assumption of the mentor role in a variety of fields. As compared with their colleagues who were not mentored, senior business executives (Roche, 1979), professors of education (Busch, 1985), and doctoral-level psychologists (Johnson, Koch, Fallow, and Huwe, 2000) who had been mentored early in their careers were found to be more likely to later sponsor protégés. Whereas these past studies have relied on retrospective accounts from individuals currently serving as mentors, this study examines the origins of mentorship reciprocity as it emerges in protégés during the initial stages of their career. Although novice geneticists are often mentored during their formative years, they are also afforded opportunities to serve as mentors themselves through their roles as teaching assistants and senior laboratory members. As such, they are an ideal population in which to examine mentorship reciprocity during the early career phase.

Developmental and Temporal Models of Mentorship. A single mentoring relationship has multiple stages that satisfy the evolving needs of a protégé (Cohen, 1995; Kram, 1985). Kram (1985) observed that there are four stages of a mentoring relationship. In the initiation phase anticipation grows, and the mentor and protégé establish mutual trust and respect. In the cultivation phase the protégé experiences a sense of equilibrium and feels support and empowerment while growing in competence and confidence. In the separation phase the protégé experiences a newfound sense of independence and autonomy. The equilibrium dissolves, and feelings of loss, turmoil, and anxiety are not uncommon. Finally, in the redefinition phase both mentor and protégé recognize that a developmental shift has occurred and that the mentorship is no longer needed. The final outcome can either be friendship and collegiality or hostility and resentment. Levinson and others (1978) also observed that as the protégé establishes independence, the mentoring relationship can turn sour. Whereas Kram and other social scientists have focused on the developmental stages that occur in a single mentoring dyad, other authors have suggested that the evolving needs of a protégé can best be met by different mentors at distinct stages of development (Bloom, 1982; Galbraith and Maslin-Ostrowski, 2000). I will explore the different developmental needs that are satisfied by mentors who come either before a geneticist begins graduate study or after a geneticist enters graduate school. I will also present data that suggest that earlier mentors may be especially important in fostering mentorship reciprocity.

Sample Description

Twenty-one geneticists were interviewed (mean age = 30, range = 26–36). Interviews with twenty journalists provided a comparison group (mean age = 24, range 21–29). Samples contained an equal number of men and women. The relatively higher mean age of the genetics sample reflects the longer training required to enter the field. We sought to interview individuals poised to become future leaders of these fields; therefore we depended on nominations when selecting participants rather than relying on a random sample. Participants were nominated as "exceptional" and "promising" by current leaders in both fields.

Method

Participants completed a semistructured, audio-recorded interview that lasted approximately two hours. The questions assessed the participants' goals, practices, values, and formative influences. They also completed two sorting tasks called "Q-sorts." These measured the relative value that participants placed on their roles as mentors and the participants' perceptions of the degree to which others in their field valued mentoring.

Analysis. Three raters coded the interview transcripts. For purposes of this study, I restricted analysis to individuals whom the participants identified as mentors during the interview. I chose to focus on mentors who were members of the professional field to which the novice aspired and were directly involved in the development of the novice. Therefore I excluded from this analysis instances in which a participant identified as a mentor either a family member or an individual admired from afar. Antimentors were defined as individuals who had a negative impact on a participant's achievement or career development. I excluded from this analysis instances in which participants spoke of an antimentor whom they had observed in the workplace or field but who had not explicitly interfered with a participant's career development or achievement. Transcripts were coded for participation in mentoring and antimentoring relationships. In order to gauge satisfaction in each field, statements in which participants commented on situations in which they had seriously considered leaving the field were identified and coded. Interrater agreement was calculated using Cohen's kappa (1960) (mean $K = .636$).

Q-Sorts. In both sorting tasks (Q-sorts), participants were given thirty cards, each of which contained one professional value (for example, "independence," "challenge"). In the first Q-sort, they were asked to sort each card in terms of its relative importance to them as a scientist. In the second Q-sort, they were asked to sort each card in terms of the importance of the value to others in their field. Participants sorted cards into one of five categories, from least important (1) to most important (5), with a preestablished number of cards per category. In the first Q-sort, the mean rating of the "teaching and mentoring" card was used as an indication of the extent to which serving as a mentor was a professional priority. In the second Q-sort, the mean rating of the "teaching and mentoring" card was used as an indication of the perceived importance of mentoring in each field.

Findings

To understand the impact of mentoring and antimentoring relationships on scientists' commitment to their field, I contrasted their experiences of mentorship with a sample of novice journalists. Differences were found in the perceptions and experiences of mentoring between the two groups. Through a one-tailed t test, geneticists ($M = 2.70$, $SD = .92$) were found to perceive "teaching and mentoring" to be a higher professional priority for members of their field than journalists did ($M = 2.22$, $SD = .81$), $t(36) = 1.68$, $p < .05$. More geneticists than journalists reported having experienced a mentoring relationship (X^2 [1, $N = 41$] $= 2.735$, $p < .10$). (In this instance, I set a relaxed alpha level of .10 because of the small number of cases being analyzed.) Significantly fewer geneticists than journalists reported being affected by antimentoring relationships (X^2 [1, N = 36] = 4.500, $p < .05$).

The tendency toward higher rates of mentoring relationships among the geneticists may be explained by the fact that these individuals had spent a relatively longer amount of time in their field. However, this explanation does not hold for antimentoring relationships. In the relatively short period of time that journalists had spent in the field, more than twice as many were affected by antimentors. Differences in early training environments in the two fields may better account for the varying rates of mentoring and antimentoring relationships.

Differences in Training Environments. Geneticists train in academic environments, where the workplace provides opportunities for mentoring activities such as teaching and advising. In contrast, formal academic training in journalism is optional. Many participants commented that the most valuable training and early work experiences traditionally occur in newsrooms, where mentorship is not necessarily an explicit mission. A young geneticist in doctoral training is required to work with at least one adviser. In contrast, journalists in the workplace may be left to seek out mentors in individuals who are not explicitly advisers and who may not see mentoring as part of their job description. Several novice journalists told us that although they looked to newsroom editors for guidance on how to develop as writers, the editors were more immediately concerned with the pressures and deadlines associated with the day-to-day operation of the news organization. Few found consistent support from editors. It is conceivable that consistent rejection and discouragement from these senior members of the newsroom may lead the novice journalist to view these individuals as antimentors.

A number of the geneticists described observing an antimentor in their graduate training institutions but managed to remain free from (in the words of one participant) "their clutches." Often geneticists were able to sample a variety of training settings by completing trial rotations in different laboratories on campus. Therefore they were able to choose graduate advisers with some prior knowledge of their management style and personality. However, in a workplace such as a newsroom, where much of a journalist's training takes place, selecting supervisors is far less common. The geneticists' relatively higher flexibility in choice of formative professional relationships may increase the likelihood that the relationships will become mentoring ones. It may also decrease the likelihood of an antimentoring relationship.

Commitment to Field and Domain. By virtue of its structure, the field of genetics may be more conducive than journalism to the development of successful mentoring relationships. This may influence the extent to which each field retains its novices. When compared with the journalists, fewer geneticists made statements indicating that they had seriously considered leaving the field (X^2 [1, N = 41] = 3.881, $p < .05$). In other words, the potential for field attrition appeared to be higher in the sample of journalists. This difference may be due in part to the significantly higher levels of experiences with antimentoring relationships in the journalism sample.

Whereas mentors are in a position to attract and retain talented young people entering a field, antimentors can discourage a young person from remaining in the field. Although on average more journalists than geneticists were negatively affected by an antimentor, the potential impact that antimentors can have on novice geneticists is still significant. A postdoctoral fellow in genetics described a verbally abusive antimentor for whom she fortunately did not work but whom she observed negatively affecting many students: "She taught me how not to supervise people. . . . Having watched her interact with her grad students and post-docs, I saw how unhappy she made them. . . . She turned a lot of very nice people, very smart people off science. That was really unfortunate."

Critical Periods of Mentoring Relationships and Levels of Mentorship Reciprocity. Geneticists often spoke at length about the valuable roles their mentors played. To study the phases of mentoring relationships, the participants' comments were coded according to the following categories: roles of mentoring relationships occurring before graduate study; roles of mentoring relationships occurring during or after graduate study; shared roles of early and later mentoring relationships. An examination of the differences between mentoring relationships occurring before and after entrance into a doctoral program revealed that earlier relationships may have increased the protégés' inclination toward mentorship reciprocity.

Roles of Pre–Graduate School Mentors. Themes that emerged in analysis of mentoring relationships occurring before graduate study indicated that these early mentors generated excitement for the protégé about an area of study and offered opportunities to work on, and in some cases publish, research.

One postdoctoral fellow recalled an undergraduate mentor whom she credits with sparking her enthusiasm for science: "He was the one that taught the really interesting courses that said, 'these are the problems, this is how we approach them' and forced us to think about how to approach them as well." Another postdoctoral fellow recalled two influential undergraduate mentors who had helped him to decide to specialize in evolutionary genetics: "I think they gave me a real sense that it was a great field to be in. The personalities in it were people worth knowing, and there was a collegiality." By exposing students to the values and practices of a domain and to the gatekeepers who constitute a field, early mentors can generate excitement about an area of study and entice a novice to join them in the field.

Roles of Later Mentors. Participants discussed how the mentors with whom they worked during or after graduate study offered them the freedom to pursue their work with relatively few constraints and taught them the interpersonal skills necessary to manage a lab and navigate the "politics" of science. One participant described a delicate balance that a graduate school mentor struck by offering him a great deal of freedom as well as support.

Although the aim of a formal education in genetics is to cultivate scientific thinking and a mastery of laboratory techniques, mentors can help teach students other less formal skills—for instance, interpersonal skills that are crucial to success in a highly collaborative field. In a particularly dramatic example, one graduate student described a time when he shared unpublished data with a powerful member of the field at a national granting agency who in turn published the data on a Web page and did not credit the student. The student became disillusioned and considered leaving the field. The support and advice of the student's mentor helped him respond to the incident and overcome his discouragement. The student said that this and other experiences had helped him understand the role a mentor can play in teaching how to negotiate one's way in a field. "By the end of this," he commented, "hopefully, not only will I be educated in how to do molecular biology but I'll be educated in how to handle myself among my peers."

Shared Roles of Early and Late Mentors. Mentors at various stages of training perform roles that include sharing their philosophies of science, helping protégés set career goals, and teaching the fundamentals of how to carry out experiments and design research. In an example of how mentors can impart their philosophy, one student reported that his undergraduate and graduate mentors taught him to view science as a means to improve the quality of human life. Mentors can also help students make crucial career decisions. One female geneticist noted, "My post-doctoral advisor was female and also had a family, and could see the whole picture of science within a context of a family in a way that men with full-time wives can't."

To summarize, early and late mentoring relationships share some roles; however, there are some stage-appropriate differences. Early mentors create research opportunities and generate excitement about an area of work, whereas late mentors offer freedom to pursue work and advice on how to conduct oneself as a member of the field. These findings support Bloom's assertion (1982) that initial mentors develop a protégé's interest and commitment in a domain and later mentors focus on skill building and mastery. The roles of graduate mentors discussed by the participants are consistent with findings reported in existing social scientific literature on mentoring (see O'Neil and Wrightsman, 2001).

Influence of Early Mentoring Relationships on Mentorship Reciprocity. Geneticists who received mentoring before they entered graduate school ($n = 10$, $M = 3.90$, $SD = .99$) valued their own roles as mentors significantly more than the geneticists who did not have pre–graduate school mentors ($n = 11$, $M = 2.82$, $SD = .87$), $t(19) = 2.65$, $p < .05$. Two explanations for the differences between these two groups will be considered:

increased difficulties in later mentoring relationships and the young scientist's evolution from advisee to colleague.

Increased Difficulties in Later Mentoring Relationships. Early mentoring relationships were described in almost exclusively positive terms. Many more difficulties were evident in the discussions of later mentoring and advising relationships. For example, some participants spoke about times when their graduate school mentors had helped them in difficult situations and later in the same interview described difficult situations that came about as a result of interactions with the same mentor.

Six situations in which participants were hesitant to label past and present advisers as mentors were also revealing. Three participants did not identify their current or past advisers as mentors and reported suspicion of the advisers' motives, commenting that they were not sure the adviser was always looking out for their best interests. Three other participants described periods when they witnessed their advisers struggling to establish their own careers. These participants discussed how these incidents made them question the individuals' ability to be a mentor and forced the participant to consider doing things differently in their own careers. However, in these six cases the participants stopped short of labeling these individuals "antimentors." Although these participants reported having found themselves in difficult situations with later advisers, the relationships were clearly not entirely negative.

Evolution from Advisee to Colleague. Findings suggest that pre–graduate school mentors are more likely to be in a position to generously share opportunities and generate excitement about the domain. In later mentoring relationships, there is often more at stake. Participants noted that conflict may arise surrounding issues such as whose ideas will determine the direction of research, how credit will be distributed in publications, and how much of the work students or fellows will be allowed to take with them when they leave to start their own laboratories. These later conflicts may arise because the novice is growing out of the advisee role and growing into the role of colleague.

One sixth-year graduate student described outgrowing the mentoring relationship with his adviser:

> I think going to graduate school, you have your formative years like you do when you are a child in some way. And I think I would have considered her my mentor up until a year and a half ago. And I think every graduate student I know including myself at some point can't stand their advisor anymore (laughs). Or, at some point they've grown beyond that relationship. Where the person that was once your mentor, you don't quite see them the same way anymore. And maybe it's a matter of you spent so much time with them. . . . So I mean, yeah, she is my mentor and, you know, I will always be thankful for her taking me into her lab and so forth, but we have a different relationship now. It's different, it's more of, more professional, you know, more, I don't look up to her as my—I guess the mentoring is over.

Another sixth-year graduate student spoke about the evolving motivation for her achievement. In high school and college, she wanted to achieve for her mentors. In the later years of graduate study, the participant reported, she had come to feel more responsible to herself than to her present adviser:

> I was very much younger when I was interacting with the other two (mentors). By definition, the gap between us was larger. A high school student and a principal. An undergraduate and a professor, the gap is still very huge. And, I'm sort of at the point where I'm almost on par or at least I should be with my advisor. Like, if [my graduate school] has done its job, come this May when I graduate, I should be intellectually on par with my advisor. So, it's harder for the mentor relationship to exist, I think.

As these two participants' comments illustrate, a novice scientist's increasing feelings of autonomy can contribute to viewing an adviser less as a mentor and more as a colleague.

What Is at Stake?

The importance of the domain of genetics—with its increasing ability to manipulate the basic building blocks of human beings—looms large in the twenty-first century (Rifkin, 1998). It is imperative that this domain continue to attract and retain talented and thoughtful future leaders capable of making crucial decisions concerning the direction of this important field and, by extension, the direction of society. The traditional role of the scientific mentor as teacher and role model of ethical behavior is under great strain from increases in public and governmental scrutiny of scientists and competition for research positions, resources, and recognition (Alberts and Shine, 1994; Djerassi, 1991; Roberts and Sprague, 1995). In spite of these new pressures, the field of genetics must again make effective mentoring and the teaching of ethical conduct a priority to ensure that the next generation of scientists can responsibly preside over the potential applications of new biological technology.

How Can Mentorship Reciprocity Be Fostered?

The findings reported in this chapter suggest that mentorship reciprocity may be bolstered by participation in a mentoring relationship during a novice's earliest experiences in a field. Given the excitement and opportunities found to be typical of early mentoring relationships, the role of a mentor can be viewed as an appealing one for young protégés to incorporate into their emerging professional identity. However, as protégés become more established in a field, mentoring relationships may lose some of their initial warmth, becoming more professional and distant. In the final phase of mentoring relationships, the main developmental task is individuation by the protégé, and this separation is potentially painful (Kram, 1985; Levinson and others, 1978).

Within the limits of a small sample, this study demonstrates that later mentoring relationships can be marked by greater complexity, ambiguity, and discomfort. In graduate school and postdoctoral mentoring relationships, there can be greater opportunities for tension, especially as protégés and mentors negotiate to divide previously shared intellectual territory. For novices who have not had the benefit of pre–graduate school mentoring and whose only exposure is during this later phase, the mentoring role may seem less appealing. For this reason these novices may choose not to become mentors.

Therefore mentors may have greater potential to be role models of mentoring if they enter novices' careers during the early period of excitement and growth rather than during the later period of individuation. As such, the potential for mentorship reciprocity is highest when the age gap between the mentor and protégé is higher, the stakes are lower, the relationship is less complex, and there is less potential for conflict.

Future research in this area would benefit from confirmation with a larger sample and studies using random samples to learn if these findings generalize beyond "exceptional" and "promising" novice scientists. Studies of additional professions could further examine formal and informal systems of mentoring. Finally, understanding of mentorship reciprocity in young professionals would be deepened through use of additional measures of mentoring practices, such as experience sampling methods or interviews with the individuals whom young professionals mentor.

This study provides evidence of the powerful role that mentors play in a novice scientist's deepening sense of commitment to a domain of study and to mentoring itself. Once students become engaged in a calling, their passion for their domain may become something that they—taking cues from their own mentors—will come to share with others.

References

Alberts, B., and Shine, K. "Scientists and the Integrity of Research." *Science,* 1994, *266*(5191), 1660–1661.

Bird, S. "Overlooked Aspects in the Education of Science Professionals: Mentoring, Ethics, and Professional Responsibility." *Journal of Science Education and Technology,* 1994, *3*(1), 49–55.

Bloom, B. "The Master Teachers." *Phi Delta Kappan,* 1982, *63*(10), 664–668.

Busch, J. W. "Mentoring in Graduate Schools of Education: Mentors' Perceptions." *American Educational Research Journal,* 1985, 22(2), 257–265.

Cohen, J. "A Coefficient of Agreement for Nominal Scales." *Educational Psychological Measurement,* 1960, *20,* 37–46.

Cohen, N. H. *Mentoring Adult Learners: A Guide for Educators and Trainers.* Malabar, Fla.: Kriger, 1995.

Csikszentmihalyi, M. *Creativity: Flow and the Psychology of Discovery and Invention.* New York: HarperCollins, 1996.

Djerassi, C. "Mentoring: A Cure for Science Bashing." *Chemical and Engineering News,* 1991, *69*(47) 30–33.

Galbraith, M. W., and Maslin-Ostrowski, P. "The Mentor Facilitating Out-of-Class Cognitive and Affective Growth." In J. L. Bess and Associates (eds.), *Teaching Alone, Teaching Together: Transforming the Structure of Teams for Teaching.* San Francisco: Jossey-Bass, 2000.

Gardner, H., Csikszentmihalyi, M., and Damon, W. *Good Work.* New York: Basic Books, 2001.

Johnson, W. B., Koch, C., Fallow, G., and Huwe, J. "Prevalence of Mentoring in Clinical Versus Experimental Doctoral Programs: Survey Findings, Implications and Recommendations." Poster presented at the annual meeting of the American Psychological Association, Washington, D.C., Aug. 2000.

Kanigel, R. *Apprentice to Genius: The Making of a Scientific Dynasty.* Old Tappan, N.J.: Macmillan, 1986.

Kram, K. *Mentoring at Work: Developmental Relationships in Organizational Life.* Glenview, Ill.: Scott, Foresman, 1985.

Levinson, D. J., and others. *The Seasons of a Man's Life.* New York: Ballantine Books, 1978.

McGinnis, R. L., "Mentors Have Consequences and Reap Returns in Academic Biochemistry." Paper presented at the annual meeting of the American Educational Research Association, Boston, Apr. 1980.

O'Neil, J. M., and Wrightsman, L. S. "The Mentoring Relationship." In S. Walfish and A. Hess (eds.), *Succeeding in Graduate School: The Career Guide for Psychology Students.* Mahwah, N.J.: Erlbaum, 2001.

Rifkin, J. P. *The Biotech Century.* Los Angeles: Tarcher, 1998.

Roberts, G. C., and Sprague, R. L. "To Compete or to Educate? Mentoring and the Research Climate." *Professional Ethics Report,* 1995, *8*(4), 1–7.

Roche, G. R. "Much Ado About Mentors." *Harvard Business Review,* 1979, *57,* 14–28.

Zuckerman, H. *Scientific Elite: Nobel Laureates in the United States.* New York: Free Press, 1977.

GREGORY C. FELDMAN is a graduate student in clinical psychology at the University of Miami.

6

This chapter examines the relationship between engagement in high school math and science classes, later academic performance, and choice of college major. Quantitative analyses are complemented by case studies of college students who exhibited high or low engagement in high school.

Continuing Motivation Beyond the High School Classroom

David J. Shernoff, Lisa Hoogstra

About one hundred years ago, Marie Curie moved to Paris to become a student in chemistry and physics, later concentrating on radioactivity for her doctorate. Upon experimenting with different elements, she detected not only that uranium was radioactive, but that uranium ore was much more radioactive than uranium itself. Curie wondered if this could be due to an unknown element invisibly existing in small concentrations. With little money, she and her husband, Pierre, worked on this question for four years in a shed that had been converted from a mortuary. By the time Pierre and Marie Curie announced the discovery of radium in 1898 and won the Nobel Prize in 1903, they had made considerable personal and financial sacrifices.

What lessons may we derive from this bit of history? For one, curiosity can be a powerful force, sometimes overwhelming even basic human desires and physical needs. More importantly from the point of view of this study,[1] human progress often stems from an accumulation of interest in a given field—that is, the purposeful desire to return to the same problem or topic again and again. From an educational perspective, continuing motivation is an important but seldom considered outcome of education (Maehr, 1976). Unlike academic achievement, it has received little attention from educational researchers.

A student's continuing interest in a topic initially encountered in the classroom is one important marker of successful learning (Jackson, 1968).

This study was supported by the National Institute on Postsecondary Education, Libraries, and Lifelong Learning (Grant #R309F70069), Barbara Schneider, principal investigator. The views expressed here are those of the authors and do not represent those of their university or granting institution.

Genuine interest in an academic subject may lead to the desire to pursue related activities for their own sake. Such intrinsic motivation has been shown to be associated with short-term increases in cognitive flexibility, conceptual learning, and self-esteem (Deci and Ryan, 1985; Lepper and Greene, 1978). Interest and the desire to learn more in a subject may also affect whether or not a student enrolls in more courses in that discipline (Harackiewicz and others, 2000). Interest can thus become an important long-term as well as short-term motivator.

Continuing motivation may become especially salient in the lives of adolescents as they reach their senior year of high school, apply to and enter college, and declare a college major. Many students choose from a variety of postsecondary institutions, a choice that is often related to their career interests and aspirations. In college many courses are required as part of a general education plan, yet each student typically chooses a field of concentration. Often students have considerable latitude in choosing their college major. For many students that choice represents their first official declaration of their intended career path. As with Marie Curie, a student's choice of concentration can be the precursor to later achievements, particularly when the choice is well matched with the student's interests.

Motivation is a complex process involving an interaction of cognitive and affective factors. We next review some of the recent work identifying and clarifying several specific aspects of student motivation, including interest, achievement goals, flow experiences, and student engagement.

The Nature of Interest

In a meta-analysis of fifty-six studies, Schiefele, Krapp, and Winteler (1992) found a positive relationship between interest and achievement, with interest accounting for an average of 10 percent of the variance in academic achievement. (Previous studies have found that, on average, the correlation between interest and achievement is .32 in math and .35 in science; see Schiefele, Krapp, and Winteler, 1992.) As Schiefele (1991) notes, however, interest is always related to specific topics, and information is acquired in particular domains. In this chapter the terms *interest* and *enjoyment,* as well as terms denoting other motivational factors, therefore refer to motivation directly tied to the content area of instruction. We chose math and science as content domains. The primary reason for our choice was the conceptual distinctness of those fields, such that a continuing interest in either math or science could reasonably be linked to the pursuit of a defined body of specializations and occupations. We would expect continuing interest in science to lead to a college major such as biology or chemistry and a continuing interest in math to lead to a major such as accounting or engineering. This expectation is consistent with Maehr's definition (1976) of continuing motivation as a return to a task (or task area) at a subsequent time, in similar or varying circumstances, without visible external pressure to do so, and when other behavior alternatives are available.

Mastery and Performance Achievement Goals

Research on achievement motivation in classrooms has focused a great deal of attention on two contrasting goal constructs: mastery goals and performance goals (for a review see Ames, 1992). Mastery goals are oriented toward learning, developing new skills, and building competence. Performance goals are directed toward ability, self-worth, and outperforming others. Harackiewicz and others (2000) found that mastery goals predicted subsequent interest and enrollment in college psychology courses but not grades. Performance goals predicted grades and long-term academic performance but not interest. Therefore interest appears to be related to mastery goals and continuing motivation in a field but not to long-term performance as measured by grades.

Enjoyment: Flow Experiences and Intrinsic Motivation

Enjoyment appears to be another important component of continuing motivation. States of intense absorption in which tasks are perceived as satisfying and often exhilarating have been documented in studies of flow experiences (Csikszentmihalyi, 1997). A state of flow is most frequently achieved when individuals stretch the limits of their abilities to meet difficult challenges (Csikszentmihalyi and Csikszentmihalyi, 1988). Flow experiences are also characterized by enjoyment of the task itself, or intrinsic motivation. In the long run, individuals who develop commitments to specific fields of interest are those who follow their sense of enjoyment in chosen activities; that is, they feel that they "want to" rather than "have to" engage in such activities (Csikszentmihalyi and Nakamura, 1989; Csikszentmihalyi, Rathunde, and Whalen, 1993).

Student Engagement in High School Classrooms

Previous work (Shernoff, Knauth, and Makris, 2000; Shernoff, Schneider, and Csikszentmihalyi, 2000) has built on Csikszentmihalyi's theory of flow to identify factors contributing to student engagement and optimal learning in academic and nonacademic classes. Although similar to flow experiences, student engagement is a unique case of flow in the following ways: it refers to enjoyment of school-specific learning processes as distinct from other types of skill-related activities, such as games or hobbies; it occurs in classrooms, which are public work settings; and motivation is positive but not necessarily heightened, as it often is in activities such as football or soccer games (Brophy, 1983). In this study we conceptualize student engagement as a combination of interest, enjoyment, and concentration (see Shernoff, Schneider, and Csikszentmihalyi, 2001). Results of previous studies (Shernoff, Knauth, and Makris, 2000; Shernoff, Schneider, and Csikszentmihalyi, 2000) indicate that students report higher levels of engagement in classroom activities when performing tasks that are perceived as relevant to their future goals, that encourage student autonomy, and that provide challenges appropriate for students' skills. Although this work has focused primarily on student engagement in specific classroom situations, there is reason to suspect that measures of engagement may be predictive of continuing interest and motivation in future academic pursuits. The enjoyment that accompanies active involvement in academic activities, particularly when relevant to students' future goals, may motivate students to seek out similar experiences as they progress through school.

This Study: Overview

In this study we first examined the classroom experience of high school students across the country. For this purpose we used the Experience Sampling Method (ESM) described by Csikszentmihalyi and Larson (1987). To better understand motivation in the classroom, we asked students how interested they were in activities, how much enjoyment they felt, and other similar questions at representative moments during math and science classes over the course of an ordinary week in school. Responses were aggregated by student and analyzed separately for experiences reported in math and science classes. We then tested the relationship of motivation in the classroom to both long-term performance and interest (choice of college major) in math and science. We expected motivational variables in high school classrooms to predict future aspirations and continuing motivation but not long-term performance (Harackiewicz and others, 2000).

Method

The data for this study come from two sources: the Alfred P. Sloan Study of Youth and Social Development (SSYSD), a national longitudinal study that investigates how students think about their lives in relationship to the future; and a three-year follow-up study of these students funded by the U.S. Department of Education's National Institute on Postsecondary Education, Libraries, and Lifelong Learning.

The Original Study. We use data from the original study (the SSYSD) to measure future aspirations and motivation in high school math and science classes.

Data Collection and Participants. A subsample from the original study was selected for the purpose of understanding continuing motivation. Students who were taking math and science classes in their senior year in high school and who participated in the ESM constituted the sample to be analyzed. This sample was 62 percent female and 38 percent male; 16 percent African American, 8 percent Asian, 10 percent Hispanic, and 64 percent white; and 7 percent low income, 14 percent working class, 35 percent middle class,

26 percent upper middle class, and 14 percent upper class (because of missing data, percentages do not total 100). There was a slight response bias due to incomplete data. Males, low-income students, and Hispanics were somewhat underrepresented in comparison with the original sample. (For further details concerning the sampling design and procedures of the SSYSD, see Csikszentmihalyi and Schneider, 2000.)

Our analyses of students' engagement in high school math and science classes were based on data from the ESM. Preprogrammed wristwatches signaled the sampled students randomly eight times each day at different intervals from 7:30 A.M. through 10:30 P.M. over the course of a typical week. Students were asked to complete a one-page self-report form each time they were signaled. The method thus provided a representative sample of each person's moods and activities for that day and week.

Participants in this study provided more than 19,000 ESM responses during the week of experience sampling. Of these, we analyzed 582 responses in math classes reported by 354 students and 625 responses in science classes reported by 324 students. These students constituted our sample for analyses of engagement in classrooms and career aspirations.

Measures. The ESM self-report forms include several semantic differential scales, such as happy-sad or active-passive, as well as several 10-point Likert scales that measure respondents' cognitive and affective states at the moment signaled. Seven ESM variables pertaining to students' motivation were selected for analysis:

Interest ("Was this activity interesting?")
Enjoyment ("Did you enjoy what you were doing?")
Concentration ("How well were you concentrating")
Future importance ("How important was the activity in relation to your future goals?")
Skill ("How would you rate your skills in the activity?")
Active involvement (which combined perceptions of being active and involved)
Mood (which included feeling happy, strong, sociable, and proud)

The two composite variables (active involvement and mood) were based on factor analyses, indicating that the variables forming the composite were part of the same global factor (for active involvement, α = .658; for mood, α = .855). Previous studies (Shernoff, Schneider, and Csikszentmihalyi, 2000, 2001) have used a composite measure of student engagement that combined interest, enjoyment, and concentration. Because each of these components was of theoretical interest, this study reports them separately.

In addition to measures derived from the ESM, information on background characteristics (gender, ethnicity), socioeconomic status, family type (traditional, single parent, blended), and academic performance were obtained from the Teenage Life Questionnaire, a modified version of the

National Education Longitudinal Study conducted from 1988 to 1994 (Ingels and others, 1994). With regard to academic performance, students were asked to report their grades in math, science, English, and history. To control for performance, we used grades in high school math courses when predicting continuing motivation in math, grades in high school science courses when predicting continuing motivation in science, and average high school grade point average when predicting overall grades in college. If students who reported high interest and enjoyment in math and science classes continued to develop their interest and perform well in college, then controlling for performance in high school would allow us to determine whether this result was due to interest and enjoyment rather than prior performance or ability.

Career aspiration measures were obtained from a career survey in which students were asked what job they expected to have in the future. Career aspirations in math included engineering, accounting, and technical fields related to math (such as computer programming). Career aspirations in science included medical doctor, other medical professional (such as dentist), other science professional (such as biologist or physicist), and science or laboratory technician. Only a small number of students expected to enter careers in technical fields. Because many of these occupations (for example, computer programming or laser technology) were consistent with an interest in either math or science, these categories were combined to form one coding category and were included in our definition of both math and science career aspirations, creating a small overlap in coding.

The Follow-Up Study. A follow-up study was conducted of SSYSD participants after they had graduated from high school. We used data from the follow-up study to measure long-term performance and continuing motivation.

Data Collection and Participants. For purposes of the current analysis, we focused on students who were high school seniors in the base year of the study and who completed interviews two years after graduating from high school, when most were in their second year of college. Additional interviews were conducted with many of these participants two to three years later, when most were college seniors or had graduated from college. Participants were interviewed by telephone and asked if they were in school or working. If in school, they were asked to identify the postsecondary institution they were attending, the degree they were pursuing (B.A., B.S., associate's), their choice of college major, and their approximate grade point average; they were also asked a variety of questions about life as a college student. One hundred eighty-four students were contacted by phone for the follow-up study. Of these, sixty-eight students had reported ESM data while in math class, and sixty-two while in science class, during their senior year of high school. These were the students who constituted the sample for our analyses of continuing motivation and long-term performance. (Fifty-six students had complete data for all variables in our model predicting math major, and fifty-three students had complete data in our model predicting science major.)

Measures. Our measure of continuing motivation was selection of a college major in science in relation to motivational variables in high school science classes and selection of a college major in math in relation to motivational variables in high school math courses. In keeping with Maehr's definition (1976), selecting a college major involves not only a "returning behavior" in an open-choice situation but also a willingness to return to the topic repeatedly and purposefully in the future. Like Harackiewicz and others' study (2000), the present investigation is one of the few studies to use a behavioral measure of continuing motivation in an educational context as opposed to self-reported measures. Students' self-reported college grades were used as the measure of long-term performance because we lacked access to college transcripts.

Case Studies. Cases were selected on the basis of two criteria: extremely high or low scores on engagement during high school math or science classes and choice of major in college (math or science versus other). We selected students who scored in the top or bottom 5 percent on a composite engagement variable (averaging interest, enjoyment, and concentration) when in high school math or science classes. We also selected students who chose college majors in science or math. (For extended profiles of these students, see Hoogstra, 2001.) The cases illustrate the association between early motivation in high school math and science classes and college outcomes in the context of students' lives.

Results

In our first analysis we attempted to predict aspirations for occupations relating to math and science from motivational variables in high school math and science classrooms. For each variable, we conducted a separate logistic regression controlling for the gender, race, socioeconomic status, family type, and performance of the student. The results are presented in Table 6.1. The only variable that predicted preference for a math career in high school was the perception that activities in math classes were important to one's future goals ($B = .274$, $p < .01$). None of the variables measured during science classes predicted career aspirations for occupations relating to science.

Next we used the same motivational variables in math and science classes measured during the senior year to predict the selection of college major in math or science. In these sets of separate logistic regressions, we were investigating whether motivational variables in high school classes would predict continuing motivation in the same field two years later after controlling for background characteristics and previous performance. We set alpha at .10 due to the small number of cases being analyzed ($N = 56$ for math, $N = 53$ for science). The results are presented in Table 6.2. None of

Table 6.1. Logistic Regression Coefficients Predicting Math and Science Career Aspirations

Variable	*Math Career*[a]	*Science Career*[b]
Interest	–0.002	0.052
Enjoyment	0.050	0.098
Concentration	0.100	0.068
Future importance	0.274*	0.104
Skill	–0.118	0.082
Active involvement	0.072	0.009
Mood	0.128	0.109

[a]The coefficient predicting aspirations for math-related careers from motivational variables in high school math classes after controlling for gender, race, socioeconomic status, family type, and performance. $N = 244$.

[b]The coefficient predicting aspirations for science-related careers from motivational variables in high school science classes after controlling for gender, race, socioeconomic status, family type, and performance. $N = 235$.

*$p < .01$.

the motivational variables in high school math classes predicted selection of a math major two years later. However, the selection of a science major in college was positively predicted by interest ($B = .836$, $p < .01$), enjoyment ($B = 1.43$, $p < .01$), and concentration ($B = 1.163$, $p < .05$), as well as by skill, active involvement, and mood, during high school science classes two years prior.

Finally, we attempted to predict college grades from motivational variables in math and science classes during the senior year. We had data on students' reports of their grades in college on average, not for each subject separately as we had in high school. We therefore combined motivational data in high school math and science classes to predict overall grades in college in separate OLS (ordinary least squares) regressions controlling for student background characteristics. The results are presented in Table 6.3. Both interest ($B = .150$, $t = 1.72$, $p < .10$) and enjoyment ($B = .133$, $t = 1.73$, $p < .10$) in math and science classes positively predicted grades in college two years later, even when controlling for high school grades. None of the other variables were significant predictors after controlling for background characteristics. In addition, although interest and enjoyment positively predicted grades in college after controlling for the other variables in the models, high school grade point average did not (in the interest model, $B = .038$, $t = .136$, n.s.; in the enjoyment model, $B = .085$, $t = .297$, n.s.).

What these results suggest is that students' experiences of interest and enjoyment in high school science classes are related to the majors they choose in college. Certainly, some students may be predisposed to major in science, but what seems noteworthy is that the experience of being cognitively and emotionally engaged with a particular topic may direct students'

Table 6.2. Logistic Regression Coefficients Predicting Math and Science Majors

Variable	*Math Major*[a]	*Science Major*[b]
Interest	–0.363	0.836***
Enjoyment	0.011	1.43***
Concentration	–0.051	1.163**
Future importance	0.150	0.227
Skill	0.120	0.916**
Active involvement	–0.197	1.116*
Mood	–0.647	2.024**

[a]The coefficient predicting selection of a college major in math from motivational variables in math classes measured two years prior, during the senior year of high school, after controlling for gender, race, socioeconomic status, family type, and previous performance. $N = 56$.

[b]The coefficient predicting selection of a college major in science from motivational variables in science classes measured two years prior, during the senior year of high school, after controlling for gender, race, socioeconomic status, family type, and previous performance. $N = 53$.

*$p < .10$. **$p < .05$. ***$p < .01$.

choices of college courses and majors. Moreover, interest and enjoyment in high school math and science classes are significant predictors of academic performance in college, whereas high school grades are not.

Case Studies

The following case studies illustrate that students reporting high engagement in high school classes sustain their interest in a particular field of study, whereas students reporting low engagement are more likely to change

Table 6.3. OLS Regression Coefficients Predicting Grades in College

Variable	*College Grades*
Interest	0.150*
Enjoyment	0.133*
Concentration	0.110
Future importance	0.040
Skill	0.052
Active involvement	–0.203
Mood	–0.124

Note: The coefficients predicting grades in college from motivational variables in math and science classes measured two years prior, during the senior year of high school, after controlling for gender, race, socioeconomic status, family type, and previous performance. $N = 75$.

*$p < .10$.

majors and career interests. We contrast two students who exhibited high engagement in their high school science classes with a third student who reported low engagement. Cases were selected on the basis of students' engagement scores in high school math or science classes, not on the basis of occupational aspirations.

Like the students in our larger sample, those selected for the case studies vary with respect to gender, race and ethnicity, family background, and socioeconomic status. As the results of our quantitative analyses indicate, however, interest and engagement remain significant predictors of continuing motivation even after accounting for background characteristics.

High Engagement. As a high school senior, Will Burton was taking honors courses in physics and math analysis and was receiving high grades in those classes. "All through [school] on all my report cards," he said, "my math and science grades [were] always highest and my English and history grades [were] always lower." He believed the reason for this difference in his performance was that his knowledge of math and science was more developed than his knowledge of other subjects and that therefore it was easier for him to grasp new concepts in math and science.

Will's favorite course was physics. Explaining the reason for this, he said, "because I'm interested in science, it's science-related, and I've always liked science." He emphasized that he liked anything related to science and commented, "I think science is going to be a basic part of my life in the future." Even at this time in his life, Will had identified a field of interest, one that mirrored his career aspirations. "Ever since at least probably freshman year," he explained, "I've always known that I wanted to go into medicine. . . . Maybe it was because . . . my second favorite [class] is bio and . . . I've always wanted to do well in that class." Will said he expected to become a pediatrician, both because of his interest in science and because he had always been good with kids.

Throughout subsequent interviews over the next five years, Will continued to demonstrate a strong interest in science. When we interviewed him during his freshman and sophomore years in college, he was pursuing a bachelor's degree in biology, maintaining a B average, and still planning to become a pediatrician. "[I]t's something that's always interested me," he remarked. "I love kids, I love medicine, and put the two together and you've got pediatrics."

Will sustained his interest in medicine throughout college. He noted that "as college went on [he] just got more and more interested in [medicine] and more and more intrigued by the whole subject." Demonstrating his continuing interest, he enrolled in a one-year medical master's program after graduating from college. The program reinforced his desire to go into medicine: "My goals were always there, but this past year kind of put them into fruition. Just . . . being in class and having actual patients come in and talking, and you know people with Alzheimer's disease, and just . . . knowing it's really real."

When we last interviewed him, Will was studying for the Medical College Admission Test, working for a doctor as a medical researcher, and planning to volunteer at a local hospital. He had made some very strategic job choices that allowed him to gain science-related work experiences outside of his graduate program.

Like Will, Elena Rodriguez received high grades and was enrolled in several advanced courses, including honors chemistry, during her senior year in high school. In describing her courses, Elena explained that she felt most challenged in her math and science classes and worked hardest in those courses. Science was her favorite subject, and she knew she wanted to pursue a degree in science, "any kind of science at all, like chemistry." Her favorite course, however, was biology because she liked "studying about animals." She noted that she was thinking of majoring in biology, or perhaps genetics, when she went to college. Her appreciation for science had been consistent throughout school. "[Even when] I had a bad teacher," she said, "I still liked it, so I could manage it." Grades motivated her only because they were the key to continued learning: "I know that if I don't graduate with good grades, then even though they are not important to me, they are important for getting into college."

Elena's engagement and self-direction were also evident five years later, although life events had substantially altered her timetable for completing her education. When interviewed at this time, Elena had married, was attending a two-year college close to home, and was majoring in biology. She had worked part-time throughout college and taken only one or two classes per semester, both for financial reasons and to maintain a high grade point average. Because of her reduced course load, she had not yet completed her associate's degree. However, she hoped that by doing well in her classes, she would be able to qualify for a scholarship to a four-year college. She explained, "I just see this school as basically the vehicle to take me further, . . . so when I transfer out I can go just two more years to a university and get my [bachelor's] degree in biology." Eventually, she said, she hoped to go on to obtain her Ph.D.

Despite financial setbacks, Elena remained committed to pursuing a degree in biology. Although she was behind schedule in completing her degree, she was receiving A's and B's in her courses, had taken several classes in her major, and was in the process of deciding on an area of specialization within biology. Like Will, her interest in science continued to motivate her to pursue her goals. (A similar case study of Elena appears in Csikszentmihalyi, Schneider, Shernoff, and Hoogstra, 2001.)

Low Engagement. During her senior year in high school, Felicia Evens was taking physics, anatomy/physiology, precalculus, English, and advanced-placement history, and was getting A's and B's in her courses. She noted that she worked hard in all her classes but felt challenged only in her math and history classes. Although she was taking two advanced courses in the sciences, she indicated that she rarely felt challenged in those classes.

Asked what type of job or career she expected to pursue after she completed her education, she said that she was thinking of going into nursing. "I like talking about the body and stuff like that," she explained. "And I can remember stuff as far as, you know, the physiology of the body and all that type of stuff. So that's why I think I'd like [nursing]." Unlike Will, however, she offered only a vague explanation for her interest in medicine and expressed none of his enthusiasm when talking about her science classes.

In contrast to Will and Elena, who remained committed to a specific field of study throughout early adulthood, Felicia's interests changed several times after high school. She initially enrolled in a four-year nursing program but disliked the nursing curriculum and felt that nursing "[didn't] pay enough." She left the program after a year to pursue an associate's degree in laboratory technology. She explained that the program appealed to her because she could complete her degree in less than two years and would then be able to work full-time. She noted that she might return to school in the future to earn a bachelor's degree in medical technology, a field related to her earlier interest in nursing, but had no firm plans to do so.

After completing her degree in laboratory technology, Felicia took a full-time job as a laboratory technician in the food industry. Asked why she was working, she said, "Why am I working? Everybody has to work. Um, to pay bills and for benefits in the future so I can get ready to think about retiring and all that good stuff." She also noted that there were a lot of opportunities for career advancement, observing, "[T]he food industry is a good, solid concrete industry. I mean we gotta eat." She expressed little interest in the content of her work and focused instead on the extrinsic rewards of her job.

By age twenty-three, Felicia had abandoned her earlier plans to return to school and study medical technology. She indicated that she was now considering pursuing a degree in microbiology, a field that would enable her to advance in the food industry. In making decisions about school and work, Felicia appeared to be motivated primarily by a desire for economic security. She gave the impression that she was working because she had to work, not because of the interest, challenge, or enjoyment that the work entailed.

Case Studies: Conclusions. These case studies suggest that interest not only influences students' choice of major but may also be an important predictor of educational persistence and career commitment. A strong interest in medicine motivated Will to develop strategies for gaining admission to medical school. A continuing interest in biology helped Elena to persist in pursuing her bachelor's degree despite numerous obstacles and setbacks. In contrast, Felicia's lack of engagement appeared to contribute to a pattern of shifting educational and occupational goals.

Analysis

Our quantitative analyses suggest that motivational variables in classrooms are generally not significant predictors of high school students' career aspirations. We believe this result is a product of the prevailing uncertainty among adolescents regarding their occupational and career plans. Our data, however, do provide some evidence that motivational variables can be a significant predictor of continuing motivation in the field of science. This applies not only to interest and enjoyment but also to concentration, active involvement, mood, and perceived skill. Interestingly, engagement in classes predicted continuing interest better than students' own career projections.

Interest and enjoyment also predicted college grades two years later. Not only were students who were more engaged in high school science classes more likely to major in science, but students who enjoyed and were interested in math and science classes performed better overall in their college classes. Among all of the variables we tested in our analyses, interest and enjoyment were among the strongest predictors of both continuing motivation in science and subsequent performance in college. This was true even when taking into account other factors, such as student background characteristics and high school grades, suggesting that these results are not due to differences in upbringing, ability, or prior performance. Contrary to the reasonable expectation that future performance is best predicted by past performance, interest and enjoyment in math and science classes appear to be stronger determinants of performance in college than high school grades are. Building on the findings of Csikszentmihalyi, Rathunde, and Whalen (1993), these results point to the importance of intrinsic motivation and optimal experiences in determining long-term motivation and commitment to a field of study.

Why these variables are strong predictors of continuing motivation in science but not math is not immediately clear. It is possible that the importance of educational engagement to continuing motivation is subject specific. It may also be the case that students who are interested in math have more difficulty identifying occupations related to their interests. Careers with an obvious relationship to math—for example, a career in "pure" math or in a strictly applied field such as accounting—are few and may have limited appeal for the majority of students who have an interest in math.

When comparing students reporting high engagement in math and science classrooms with those reporting low engagement, we found that the highly engaged students frequently spoke about liking their favorite subjects and being interested in them. For highly engaged students, in contrast to students reporting low engagement, their interest and enjoyment in specific fields were fundamental considerations when thinking about their future and making important decisions about college, area of specialization, and possible careers. Students who reported low engagement appeared more concerned with their performance, their grades, and other external indicators of success. Interestingly, the students who reported low engagement did not fit the stereotype of underachievement and indifference. On the contrary, many were highly ambitious and concerned with their performance.

The student interviews helped to illustrate how mastery goals and performance goals operate in the real lives of adolescents. It is important to keep in mind that even intrinsically motivated individuals with strong mastery goals live in a highly competitive society and may seek to participate in competitive fields. Therefore performance goals may often be necessary and important in the pursuit of intrinsically interesting questions and topics. To some extent, students reporting high and low engagement exhibited both mastery and performance goals but gave them different emphasis. For Will and Elena concerns about performance appeared to be secondary to their interest in science. Success was important to the extent that it enabled them to pursue degrees and careers related to their interests. For Felicia the emphasis was reversed. Her concerns about mastery were subordinate to her concerns with performance. She valued competence and skill building as means to an end—a secure job with opportunities for career advancement.

Although intrinsic interest in a subject may enhance long-term performance, as demonstrated by the higher college grades of students who exhibited an interest in math or science in high school, an overemphasis on grades, tests, and other measures of performance may have the effect of reducing student interest and engagement. This study suggests that teachers who desire to nurture lifelong learners would be wise to focus on creating the conditions that allow students' natural interest and enjoyment in a subject to develop. Teachers obviously have a professional duty to be concerned with short-term learning gains and to evaluate those gains. One key to the lasting success of students, however, appears to be authentic engagement, including genuine interest in and enjoyment of a topic.

Note

1. Data for the study, including all quotations, were derived from two sources: (1) the Alfred P. Sloan Study of Youth and Social Development (principal investigators Charles Bidwell, Mihaly Csikszentmihaly, Larry Hedges, and Barbara Schneider), and (2) a three-year follow up study funded by the U.S. Department of Education's national Institute on Postsecondary Education, Libraries, and Lifelong Learning (principal investigator Barbara Schneider). Permission to use these studies as data sources was granted by the principle investigators. Written consent to participate was obtained from parents of each young participant in the study, and verbal consent was obtained from each participant. Quotations for case studies were taken from tape-recorded interviews. Under the guidelines of the University of Chicago Institutional Review Board, the confidentiality of all information obtained from participants has been maintained since the project's inception. Pseudonyms have been used for all participants, and sensitive information was excluded.

References

Ames, C. "Classrooms: Goals, Structures, and Student Motivation." *Journal of Educational Psychology*, 1992, *84*(3), 261–271.

Brophy, J. E. "Conceptualizing Student Motivation." *Educational Psychologist*, 1983, *18*(3), 200–215.

Csikszentmihalyi, M. *Finding Flow: The Psychology of Engagement with Everyday Life.* New York: Basic Books, 1997.

Csikszentmihalyi, M., and Csikszentmihalyi, I. S. (eds.). *Optimal Experience: Psychological Studies of Flow in Consciousness.* New York: Cambridge University Press, 1988.

Csikszentmihalyi, M., and Larson, R. "Validity and Reliability of the Experience-Sampling Method." *Journal of Nervous and Mental Disease,* 1987, *175*(9), 525–536.

Csikszentmihalyi, M., and Nakamura, J. "The Dynamics of Intrinsic Motivation: A Study of Adolescents." In R. Ames and C. Ames (eds.), *Research on Motivation in Education.* Orlando, Fla.: Academic Press, 1989.

Csikszentmihalyi, M., Rathunde, K., and Whalen, S. *Talented Teenagers: The Roots of Success and Failure.* New York: Cambridge University Press, 1993.

Csikszentmihalyi, M., and Schneider, B. *Becoming Adult: How Teenagers Prepare for the World of Work.* New York: Basic Books, 2000.

Csikszentmihalyi, M., Schneider, B., Shernoff, D., and Hoogstra, L. "Preparing for the World of Work." *NAMTA Journal,* 2001, *26*(1), 123–138.

Deci, E. L., and Ryan, R. M. *Intrinsic Motivation and Self-Determination in Human Behavior.* New York: Plenum, 1985.

Harackiewicz, J. M., and others. "Short-Term and Long-Term Consequences of Achievement Goals: Predicting Interest and Performance over Time." *Journal of Educational Psychology,* 2000, *92*(2), 316–330.

Hoogstra, L. "Divergent Paths After High School: Predictors of Successful and Unsuccessful Transitions to College and Work." Unpublished doctoral dissertation, Committee on Human Development, University of Chicago, 2001.

Ingels, S. J., and others. *National Education Longitudinal Study of 1988, Second Follow-Up: Student Component Data File User's Manual.* Washington, D.C.: U.S. Department of Education, National Center for Education Statistics, 1994.

Jackson, P. W. *Life in Classrooms.* Austin, Tex.: Holt, Rinehart and Winston, 1968.

Lepper, M. R., and Greene, D. *The Hidden Costs of Reward: New Perspectives on the Psychology of Human Motivation.* Mahwah, N.J.: Erlbaum, 1978.

Maehr, M. L. "Continuing Motivation: An Analysis of a Seldom Considered Educational Outcome." *Review of Educational Research,* 1976, *46*(3), 443–462.

Schiefele, U. "Interest, Learning, and Motivation." *Educational Psychologist,* 1991, *26*(3–4), 299–323.

Schiefele, U., Krapp, A., and Winteler, A. "Interest as a Predictor of Academic Achievement: A Meta-Analysis of Research." In K. A. Renninger, S. Hidi, and A. Krapp (eds.), *The Role of Interest in Learning and Development.* Mahwah, N.J.: Erlbaum, 1992.

Shernoff, D. J., Knauth, S., and Makris, E. "The Quality of Classroom Experiences." In M. Csikszentmihalyi and B. Schneider (eds.). *Becoming Adult: How Teenagers Prepare for the World of Work.* New York: Basic Books, 2000.

Shernoff, D. J., Schneider, B., and Csikszentmihalyi, M. "Optimal Learning Experiences: Understanding Student Engagement in High School Classrooms." Unpublished manuscript, 2000.

Shernoff, D. J., Schneider, B., and Csikszentmihalyi, M. "Assessing Multiple Influences on Student Engagement in High School Classrooms." Paper presented at the American Educational Research Association Conference, Seattle, Apr. 2001.

DAVID J. SHERNOFF is a doctoral student in education and human development at the University of Chicago.

LISA HOOGSTRA is a doctoral student in human development at the University of Chicago.

INDEX

OTHER TITLES AVAILABLE IN THE NEW DIRECTIONS FOR CHILD AND ADOLESCENT DEVELOPMENT SERIES
William Damon, Editor-in-Chief

CD92 The Role of Family Literacy Environments in Promoting Young Children's Emerging Literacy Skills, *Pia Rebello Britto, Jeanne Brooks-Gunn*
CD91 The Role of Friendship in Psychological Adjustment, *Douglas W. Nangle, Cynthia A. Erdley*
CD90 Symbolic and Social Constraints on the Development of Children's Artistic Style, *Chris J. Boyatzis, Malcolm W. Watson*
CD89 Rights and Wrongs: How Children and Young Adults Evaluate the World, *Marta Laupa*
CD88 Recent Advances in the Measurement of Acceptance and Rejection in the Peer System, *Antonius H. N. Cillessen, William M. Bukowski*
CD87 Variability in the Social Construction of the Child, *Sara Harkness, Catherine Raeff, Charles M. Super*
CD86 Conflict as a Context for Understanding Maternal Beliefs About Child Rearing and Children's Misbehavior, *Paul D. Hastings, Caroline C. Piotrowski*
CD85 Homeless and Working Youth Around the World: Exploring Developmental Issues, *Marcela Raffaelli, Reed W. Larson*
CD84 The Role of Peer Groups in Adolescent Social Identity: Exploring the Importance of Stability and Change, *Jeffrey A. McLellan, Mary Jo V. Pugh*
CD83 Development and Cultural Change: Reciprocal Processes, *Elliot Turiel*
CD82 Temporal Rhythms in Adolescence: Clocks, Calendars, and the Coordination of Daily Life, *Ann C. Crouter, Reed W. Larson*
CD81 Socioemotional Development Across Cultures, *Dinesh Sharma, Kurt W. Fischer*
CD80 Sociometry Then and Now: Building on Six Decades of Measuring Children's Experiences with the Peer Group, *William M. Bukowski, Antonius H. Cillessen*
CD79 The Nature and Functions of Gesture in Children's Communication, *Jana M. Iverson, Susan Goldin-Meadow*
CD78 Romantic Relationships in Adolescence: Developmental Perspectives, *Shmuel Shulman, W. Andrew Collins*
CD77 The Communication of Emotion: Current Research from Diverse Perspectives, *Karen Caplovitz Barrett*
CD76 Culture as a Context for Moral Development, *Herbert D. Saltzstein*
CD75 The Emergence of Core Domains of Thought: Children's Reasoning About Physical, Psychological, and Biological Phenomena, *Henry M. Wellman, Kayoko Inagaki*
CD74 Understanding How Family-Level Dynamics Affect Children's Development: Studies of Two-Parent Families, *James P. McHale, Philip A. Cowan*
CD73 Children's Autonomy, Social Competence, and Interactions with Adults and Other Children: Exploring Connections and Consequences, *Melanie Killen*
CD72 Creativity from Childhood Through Adulthood: The Developmental Issues, *Mark A. Runco*
CD69 Exploring Young Children's Concepts of Self and Other Through Conversation, *Linda L. Sperry, Patricia A. Smiley*
CD67 Cultural Practices as Contexts for Development, *Jacqueline J. Goodnow, Peggy J. Miller, Frank Kessel*
CD65 Childhood Gender Segregation: Causes and Consequences, *Campbell Leaper*
CD46 Economic Stress: Effects on Family Life and Child Development, *Vonnie C. McLoyd, Constance Flanagan*
CD40 Parental Behavior in Diverse Societies, *Robert A. LeVine, Patrice M. Miller, Mary Maxwell West*